ORDINARY PEOPLE, EXTRAORDINARY LIVES

How to Dream, Believe and Achieve
whatever you want.

Michael Winegarden

BALBOA.
PRESS
A DIVISION OF HAY HOUSE

Balboa Press books may be ordered through booksellers or by contacting:

Balboa Press
A Division of Hay House
1663 Liberty Drive
Bloomington, IN 47403
www.balboapress.com
1 (877) 407-4847

Because of the dynamic nature of the Internet, any web addresses or links contained in this book may have changed since publication and may no longer be valid. The views expressed in this work are solely those of the author and do not necessarily reflect the views of the publisher, and the publisher hereby disclaims any responsibility for them.

The author of this book does not dispense medical advice or prescribe the use of any technique as a form of treatment for physical, emotional, or medical problems without the advice of a physician, either directly or indirectly. The intent of the author is only to offer information of a general nature to help you in your quest for emotional and spiritual well-being. In the event you use any of the information in this book for yourself, which is your constitutional right, the author and the publisher assume no responsibility for your actions.

Any people depicted in stock imagery provided by Thinkstock are models, and such images are being used for illustrative purposes only.
Certain stock imagery © Thinkstock.

Print information available on the last page.

ISBN: 978-1-5043-4482-1 (sc)
ISBN: 978-1-5043-4483-8 (hc)
ISBN: 978-1-5043-4481-4 (e)

Library of Congress Control Number: 2015918708

Balboa Press rev. date: 01/26/2016

CONTENTS

ACKNOWLEDGMENTS

There are a number of people I would like to acknowledge. These people are all indirectly responsible for the writing of this book but who have impacted me deeply in my life and learning and it is that learning that spawned this book and all that I do.

To my Mom and Dad. I have no idea what I could have ended up being like without your teachings. It was through your actions I learned my core values. Honesty, integrity and ethics.

To my Uncle Bill Murphy. Such a kind gentle man with the right amount of advice and wisdom when I needed it along with a homemade Murphy burger and beer when I needed that too. The verbal kicks in the seat of one's pants didn't hurt either.

I learned so much from so many during those trying college days. Through their dedication I learned passion and many other things. Judy Hart, Rick Casey, Bob Wall, Bob Evans and so many more.

Janice Stevens. You hired me for my first job 18 years ago and understood I had to do things differently. After all those years we found each other again and we have come together to finish this book and to share our lives. This is just more proof the universe is a remarkable wondrous place to make our dreams come true.

Warren Bechard. I still tell stories about my co-op placement with you. I learned a lot including the point of the old bull young bull joke.

My best friend Glen. There is too much to say. Thank you.

My boys. I am proud of you and love you very much.

There are so many great minds who are gone now. They all touched me and I think made a difference in my life.

Uncle Ken Winegarden. Like your brother my dad, your humour and intelligence gave me many smiles and things to ponder over the years.

George Barney. My war hero math teacher who was a pilot first and a teacher second. We will meet again. Rest in peace my friend.

To so many I will never be able to shake hands with or hug who have given me the opportunity to read their written words for all of us to study. Whose message I will pledge to try to carry on to the next generation of wonderful people and help them learn to dream, believe and achieve what they want. Some of these people are still with us and I hope to have you on my stage sharing your knowledge and entertaining the people who are hungry for the information we have to give. Dale Carnegie, Earl Nightingale, Napoleon Hill, Bob Proctor, Bob Doyle, Gary Craig, and so many more.

I have read various biographies and auto biographies and learned something from each of them.

Thank you to all the people who have touched my life in various ways. You all had something to do with helping me become the person I am today and it is that person who was able to write this book.

Michael E. Winegarden
http://www.loasecret.com

INTRODUCTION

This book has one main purpose. To teach you the techniques to live your life by design. To dream, believe and achieve what you want. To show you how to be successful in whatever you want. Most importantly, to have a happy life, no matter what your current situation is. Yes even to live a life of passion.

In the pages of this book, you will find what some call the secrets to success. It took me years of searching, a great deal of money and a lot of time to discover these secrets. This book details what I have learned and will teach you everything you need to know to make a very big difference in your life.

You can do this! You can make the difference in your life and help others around you. It doesn't matter what your level of education is; it doesn't matter how much money you have; it doesn't even matter if you have a disability or anything else real or perceived that has held you back. I do have a few major disabilities myself. I am totally blind and have less than half my hearing. I have hands that were destroyed in my previous job. But what I also have is a strong desire to learn and grow; a need to be all I can be; a burning desire to reach levels of success that no-one ever thought I would or even could. Throughout my life, I have never given up

I did get beaten down along the way and eventually when I picked myself up, I put it all together. I learned what I was doing wrong and I learned what worked. I read many books and studied many programs. I studied people who I met throughout my life and I finally figured it out. Once I did, things totally changed in my life forever.

I will never live in fear again. I will never be alone. I will always be happy and I will always enjoy life. I will always live in love!

If this sounds like something you have heard before or the old saying 'It's too good to be true' then I am sorry. Sorry that you are still searching and I trust that your search has now ended.

I have written in this book all you will ever need to know to do, have or become anything you want. I have written it in simple terms so that you can easily grasp my teaching. I hope you enjoy the learning process that you are about to begin.

Did you know that the world has a huge problem? A vast percentage of us live in lower to middle class? Way too many of us live in poverty? So many aren't happy with their overall lives? So many dreams are unfulfilled? So many are looking for love, driving a car they don't like or living in a place they'd rather not be in? Many are stuck in an unsatisfying job just to pay the bills and yet still can't make ends meet. Some are just not feeling very happy or are not enthusiastic about life and just don't know why. I know how this feels, I was one of them.

You have in your possession right now, the answers to all these things. It is my goal to teach as many people as possible how to be successful and live their dreams. That's what this book is all about; to teach you, yes you, how to dream, believe and achieve whatever you want. Big promise?

I do realize that this may sound unbelievable to some people. I understand sceptics; to some degree I was one. No longer! I have proven that this works. I have passed on my knowledge to others who are also getting success and living a happier life.

Will you take this information, apply it and reach levels of high success? I do not know the answer to this question. I can only provide you with the information and it is totally up to you to take the time to make the difference in your life.

You are very likely going to be faced with information you have never heard before. You may even think that this information is strange. Food for thought - if you want things in your life to change then you need to change things in your life. You simply can't go on doing everything as you always have and expect a different result. That is just common sense.

I am blind and I can't hear well either. I wasn't supposed to be successful but I just wouldn't give up, at least not for long. Something told me to keep learning. I had to expand my mind with new knowledge. My story will unfold throughout this book.

The sad thing in the world today is that a high percentage of people never get ahead. I have read that over 90% of people die with almost no money in the bank. The actual number I heard was close to 98%. That is just in North America; other parts of the world are even higher. Worse yet, most of those people have not experienced or ever touched their dreams. How sad.

This means that all their lives, they were nothing more than slaves to the system. They worked all their lives for what? To end up with nothing and empty dreams! This breaks my heart.

I decided that I wasn't going to be one of these people. I knew there had to be a better way. I knew that if I thought the way everyone else did then I would be just like them. I had to open my mind. I had to learn things that others didn't know. In the following pages I will share with you all of my knowledge so you don't have to end up being one of the 98%.

I struggled, I mean really struggled. I had everything going against me. At the time of writing this book, I am still blind and over half deaf. I say this because I do plan on seeing and hearing again normally. I have been this way since my childhood. We all have our stories but I made it. I did it. Most importantly, I will continue to make it and fulfill all of my dreams.

So I can do it and have done it. Now it's your turn. It is your time to shine. I hold nothing back in this book because I want, no, I need you to succeed. This is my passion, my driving purpose. I must teach you how to get all the things you want and to become who and what you want to be. It is possible and you can do it.

I will show you how to attract amazing things. I will explain everything as simply as I can and in as much detail as you need. You can have that fancy car if that's what you really want. You can meet the love of your life if that's what you want. You can have more money. You can be the greatest at anything you want to be; a teacher, firefighter, florist, musician, wealthy, etc. Most importantly, of course, is for you to feel good. To be able to enjoy your life the way you really can and should.

I want you to think of your time reading this book as a learning journey. You need to honour your time with me. There will be things that you must learn and actions you will need to take. If you skip over any of this information or rush through it, you won't get the results you deserve. I encourage you to take your time, really understand this information and apply it in your life so you too can make a difference.

You need to read this book many times because you are learning new concepts that take practice to master. You can't possibly understand all the information I am giving you just by reading it once or twice. Keep this book close by you. Every time you read it, you will understand at a higher level.

It is when you reach that higher level that you will be able to make very real differences in your life.

Now I pull back the curtains and welcome you inside.

Michael E Winegarden

CHAPTER 1

Choose Success

The information that I am about to share with you has been around for a long time. In fact, it has been there since the beginning of time. After you have learned what I am teaching you, you will be able to see how famous people throughout time have used it to become the best in their field. Be it the rich and famous, brilliant musicians, sports stars, world leaders who have made amazing differences, leaders of industry, or those who have held monopolies. My research shows that people have known about this information for generations. 'They' have tried to keep this information to themselves; in fact some even believe that it is genetic and not learned behaviour. This is silly.

The wealthiest and most successful people know this information. Those who live in an ongoing state of bliss know this information, and they have learned it either directly from someone who shared this knowledge or, in some cases, figured it out by themselves.

Things have changed in the world since the internet was introduced. We can now share information more easily than before and secrets have been exposed. The world has opened up in ways that we could have never imagined. In some respects, we are all on a more equal playing field.

Just by clicking a few links on a screen, we can now access information that was not readily available before. We can read books that were written many years ago. In these books, we can find some of the information that has been explained here; information that previously may have been found in a library or only available to those who knew about it. If it wasn't for the internet, I would not have been able to discover this information and do all the amazing things that I have done.

I can and have coached people around the world right from my chair. I can hear their voice; I can share their successes, and I find this so wonderfully exciting.

The problem is this. If you weren't born in a wealthy family, if you didn't have the opportunity to be mentored by a leader or by chance came across this information, then you are probably just like many others. You are probably living a life of mediocrity at best and poverty at worst. You are probably just like I was.

Of course, the downside to the ease of information sharing is this. There is a lot of incorrect information out there. As simple as it is to share good information, it's just as easy to share bad information. There's also incomplete information. While it might sound good, it will keep you stuck right where you are.

One of these books I am referring to was released in the last few years. It was very successful in that it achieved a lot of sales. But while some people I know got some success from following its teachings, there was nothing really life changing. There are lots of reasons for this. In fairness to the book, some people simply didn't implement everything the book stated. They just didn't study everything in the book and apply what they learned.

I too read this book along with many others. I felt that it was missing information. Some of the key elements are simply not there no matter how hard you look. One of the things I insist that people must learn is the 4 Keys. Some of these I learned from a book, others I learned from people I have met over the years.

The 4 keys themselves will not change your life. However, if you learn and apply these 4 Keys consistently, you will change your life. The rest of the information will be useless if you do not apply the 4 Keys. I will teach you about these Keys in Chapter 4.

I want to share one more thing right now that will stop you dead in your tracks. Never ever put timelines on any of your dreams. You will learn more about this as you go through this book. If you have a dream and you feel that you have to achieve it by a certain date, you will be stressed. You never want to feel stress. I have read in several books that you should have a timeline or a due date for something to happen and I totally disagree.

There are other things that I am sure you have read in other books or programs that I know have stopped you from achieving your dreams. If this is the first book that you have read on how to dream, believe and achieve whatever you want, you are very fortunate. Because you won't have to unlearn some of the things you may have picked up so far. You will also be able to make a difference in your life so much easier and more quickly than you could have ever imagined.

Clearly for many, they are not living a life of their dreams. They just aren't happy in their day to day lives. They don't feel good. Lots of people I knew had a life that they felt was unsatisfactory, me included. In fact, especially me! I had a strong desire to learn how to make my life more enjoyable. I wanted to feel good all the time and to make my dreams come true.

Once I figured out how to do this, then it became my passion. I now want to teach everyone how to make their dreams come true. Yes, my driving purpose is to put together the best information I can so that you can make your dreams become a reality. So you also can dream, believe and achieve anything you want.

It is now the crunch time. It is decision time. Are you going to choose to continue reading this book and dream, believe and achieve what you want? If you take action now and learn all I have to teach, you can do just that.

Many people buy a book or program and never read it once. These are the people who will never make a difference in their lives, much less have a positive impact on other people's lives. Please don't be one of those people. So many have good intentions but just don't follow through. Again, I ask you, don't be one of these people.

I can't say I like the term winners and losers. I think it's really quite rude to think of people in that context but I will use it here to illustrate my point.

A loser is one who buys information and doesn't even learn what they paid for. Also one who has a great idea and doesn't take action. The loser is one who finds excuses for everything in their life. Oh I don't have time to read a book. I don't have time to go to the gym. I am too tired. I'd rather watch TV than spend that very same time learning information to change my life. These people will always be a loser. They will never change a thing. They will be one of the 98% who never achieve their dreams.

A winner takes charge of their life. They decide that they will do what it takes to learn what they need to know. A winner will ignore their TV, shut off their emails, stop texting, and posting on Facebook. They will block out uninterrupted time every day to sit and learn this information. Winners prioritize the important things in their lives. This is not time management. I call it priority management. This is when you decide what is a priority and do it no matter what it takes. It is the most important item on your list of things to do that day.

Winners are the ones who will give up something they enjoy to change their lives. They are the ones who will succeed and make their dreams a reality. Winners are those who WILL dream, believe and achieve exactly what they want.

I really want you to be a winner but I can only give you the information. You need to take it and follow through. I ask you to please, be a winner.

Read my information. You must not just read it but master it. Read this book a hundred times. I am not exaggerating, 100 times. Apply it. Get the results that you deserve. I know you deserve it.

One more thing I want to encourage you to do. Perhaps more correctly, here is what I don't want you to do. Do not read a bunch of programs or books. Focus on everything in this book first. Really master this information. Then you can read other books. I will let you know about some really good books when you are ready. Just make sure you learn this information first. I have worked with people previously who made this mistake and they are just going around in circles.

They begin to learn from one person. They get a bit of information but don't master it. Then they jump to another person. They may get some other information but they don't get any closer to their dreams because they are jumping from one to another and not mastering anything. I have told my students that I won't work with them if they study someone else at the same time. The reason is simple. I don't want to have to undo the bad information that they pick up from someone else to get them back on the right track. It's a waste of time, their time and mine.

Here is more about how I figured it out.

Around 2006 I started learning about Law of Attraction. It was a totally new concept to me. My skeptic mind screamed that this was just weird. The larger part of me knew I had to look into this more.

I bought an expensive program and studied it but somehow I wasn't getting it. I knew this would help me be the person I wanted to be but yet it just wasn't working for me. So I left it alone for a while then I bought another program. It had a different spin on it. Ok, I started to get the concepts but still had no real results. This went on for some years. Then it hit me.

The problem is that the full recipe wasn't being given. I needed to go through my information and pull it together. This is when I finally got it. I dropped some things because I didn't see how it would be helpful. I included other things because I knew it would be helpful. I kept putting the various pieces of the puzzle together until I had what I believed is the complete solution.

I began applying what I thought was the correct method and things started happening. I refined the way I was doing things and got even better results. I went back to my library of materials and read through some new books and re-read other books. I listened to interviews that I had on my computer collecting digital dust. I started to realize that there was a theme coming out. I was finally getting it.

I then joined a private group on Facebook that included people with the same passion. I did this because I knew I needed to talk to people who shared my interest because no-one I knew locally was interested. I ended up being more of a facilitator than just a participant. I made some good friends and we keep in touch today. It was these folks who started calling me Magic Michael. I will always love these people for they gave me a chance to start teaching what I knew. They gave me the opportunity to share my information. Some of them have reviewed this book, and the ones closest to me are so proud of all the things I have achieved in such a short time. I will say it here, "I love you my friends from that group."

Now I have the recipe that works and more importantly, I have proof that it works. So I can teach it and make another dream of mine come true. That dream is to get this book in your hands, have an online presence, travel the world and give seminars to as many people as possible. I will make a huge difference. I will love, laugh and enjoy every bit of it. I hope you decide to be one of the 2% of people who will dream, believe and achieve whatever you want.

Dream, believe and achieve whatever you want.

CHAPTER 2

Overcoming Obstacles

I start my day the same way. I wake in the morning feeling good. It doesn't matter where I am. I have love in my heart and a smile on my face. I occasionally enjoy a morning cup of tea and a little workout in my gym. A shower and I am ready for whatever joys the day will give me.

I enjoy my mornings very much. At least I do now. No, it wasn't always like this. Not by a long shot.

Sometimes I look back on my previous life and am forced to ask some questions. Did I make a difference? Did I matter? Would anything have changed if I wasn't there? I'm not so sure. For the most part, I would say I did my best. That at least was always my intention. What was I? Was I ever really happy? Did I feel like jumping out of bed in the morning to take on and explore the wonders of this new day? If I didn't change my life how would it have ended? When I was getting to the point of being an old man and looking back on my life would I have done so with pride or excuses? In my mind, I have no doubt what the answer would have been and it would have been an unsatisfactory response.

I was born with an eye disease called Retinitis Pigmentosa that took some of my hearing as well. I never had full sight but I could see well enough to ride my beloved bicycle until around age nine.

I only had tunnel vision, meaning I never had side vision. It would be the same as looking through a narrow tube. I was always night blind but could see well enough when there was a lot of light. I guess, looking back, perhaps this was helpful in adapting to being blind in a few years.

I couldn't see well enough to play sports although I was reasonably athletic. In those days, I had big thick glasses that were quite heavy. I suppose I must have looked dorky. Come to think of it, I probably was dorky too. I didn't have a lot of friends in my first few years of school and I am sure I was called a lot of names because I couldn't join in all the reindeer games.

Some teachers in the public schools would get frustrated with me. They would drag my desk up to the blackboard and make me sit there just because I couldn't see when there was only a few lights on in the room. I would just clam up and say to heck with that! I will say that other teachers did all they could to work with me and I have never forgotten those wonderful people.

I lost a year or two of schooling because of all these issues, bearing in mind that this was way before computers. Accessibility probably wasn't even a word used back then.

As I was a pretty easy target, I was bullied. My big brother took care of a lot of that for me. I believe he used to give them a thumping and say you can't pick on Michael, he's my punching bag. My brother always did have a good sense of humour!

When I was in grade 1 or 2, I remember one winter evening when it was totally dark. I must have been kept after school for some reason and had quite a long walk home. By the time I was a few blocks away I couldn't see anything in the dark between the street lights. I was pretty scared. Probably the first time I remember feeling totally blind.

Mom sent my brother out to find me and when he came along I was stomping my boots so I could hear the sound of my feet on the sidewalk. I guess I was thinking that as long as I was on the sidewalk then I would be fine. I can't remember if I was crying but I was sure happy to hear my brother's voice. He is a few years older than I am. He said, "pretty smart kid, stomping your feet like that." Well that's all I could think of to do.

We didn't know why I wasn't able to see well until I was around 9 years old. I remember spending a whole day in a hospital having various eye tests. That was an awful day. But sometime after that the eye doctor told my folks that not only was there nothing they could do but that, in all likelihood, I was going to go blind.

The day that Dad decided it was time to take my bike away was hard on him. The doctor told him a couple of years previously to take it away. I loved my bike. That thing was my motorcycle and horse all rolled into one. Dad told the doctor that he wouldn't take it away until he had to. One day when I was around 9 or 10, Dad and I were racing. I didn't see the school wall … crash! Yep, it was time.

May I also apologise to all the little old ladies I ran into during those days. Sunlight played hell with my limited vision.

By the time I was in grade 2 or 3, I was too blind to see the blackboard and was having trouble reading books. Near the beginning of grade 5, I was placed at a school for the blind. This was a boarding school. I hated that part of it.

I really do believe that most of the staff did their best to make it enjoyable but I didn't do very well there. To say I hated it all the time is foolish. But there were many times when I would have preferred to be home in my own bed.

I was lucky though because I got to go home every weekend. Some of the kids lived too far away from the school and only got to go home during longer vacations. Dad was great too. He would drive me to school Monday mornings so I could sleep one more night at home. The other students were bussed back on Sunday evenings.

I made a few lifelong friends there. I even kept in touch with a couple of the teachers too. My war hero math teacher, who has passed on now, taught me above all else to be successful as a blind person I would have to work twice as hard as the sighted folks. He sure was right! Then there was my music teacher. I call him Uncle Bill. He could see in my eyes when I was having enough of life at the school and he would get me out of there for an evening of homemade burgers and conversation. We keep in touch even today. Uncle bill has been one of my biggest supporters. Even though he has questioned a few of my choices over the years, he knew I would land on my feet. There were many others of course but then this isn't just about who I knew during my school days.

Times at the school for the blind were often quite interesting. We bent a lot of the rules. I think we changed the law of gravity once or twice too. We weren't bad kids; usually we were just having fun. Even some of the staff had a hard time disciplining us. They were laughing too hard at our antics.

Some of the things we did were simply crazy when I look back on it now. I don't know how we didn't get seriously hurt or worse.

Sometimes we used to put on roller skates in the evenings. I couldn't hear well enough to know where the walls were so I skated with either Glen or Rod. Yes, my guides while whipping around that gym were both blind. One night the staff put on some music. I stopped. Glen asked me if I was alright. I asked if he could hear the walls over the music. He laughed and off we went just like before. Man!

These guys that can hear learned to judge distances from the echo off various obstacles. They then knew it was time to turn. All this while avoiding other skaters and over the music too. I didn't think much about it at the time but it must have been impressive to watch.

I found it difficult to participate in most of the sports at that school. I couldn't see, which is fine, because neither could most of the other students. The real killer was that I couldn't hear that well either. I wore hearing aids in both ears. Since most of our sports were modified to use hearing, I was at a disadvantage. We played ice hockey, football, and even a sort of baseball.

We also competed against other "normal" schools in wrestling, swimming, and various long distance running events. I was a good swimmer but I didn't compete. I didn't care for swimming that much. I used to join the swim team for some workouts in the beginning of their season to get in shape for wrestling which started later. The swim coach kept pushing me to join the team since he claimed I was beating everyone else. That's why I didn't like swimming; I can't tell if I am winning or not. With wrestling I always knew.

I ended up with knee trouble that made running or even just walking painful a lot of the time. The wrestling coach wouldn't allow me to do something in place of running so off the team I went. Too bad, I was one of the better wrestlers. I guess he thought that I was just trying to get out of running. Some days I could run for miles with no pain but on other days one lap around the track was extremely painful.

I had tests done on my knee to try to understand what the problem was. It wasn't until I was in my early twenties when I figured it out. Glen and I started lifting weights and my knee got better. Even to this day, I hardly ever feel even a twinge from that knee. It must have been weak muscles and when they were stronger the pain just went away. So much for medical knowledge!

I've only had light perception since around the age of 10. I can only see the difference between night and day; no colours, shadows or even shapes. I have no usable vision. My eyes are light sensitive too so I wear sunglasses whenever I leave home. It's not so bad. The shades do make me look pretty cool!

After I graduated from the school for the blind I didn't know what to do. I bummed around for a year and finally my best friend Glen from the blind school and I decided to go to college and get a business diploma.

To say those days were extremely hard would be an understatement. I wasn't a good student in high school and computers and scanning technology were in their infancy so this multiplied our workload dramatically. In those days, it would take one to two minutes to scan one page. Often the page wouldn't come out readable so I had to change the settings and do it again. Hours and hours of work just to read one book!

To explain what I mean … we would get our books like everyone else in print. Then we had to scan each page and convert the books to an electronic file. This made it possible for us to read them on our computers. The text books would have different colours and the font would change. This was very difficult for the scanning software to convert accurately. I remember at least one book that just wouldn't scan so Mom typed the chapters that we needed. Crazy!

Our computers had a screen reading software that reads the text through a speaker or headphones. I still use this same method today. Programs and computers have increased in speed and are easier to understand of course but the basics are still the basics. I can't see the screen so I listen to the information.

Again I met some amazing staff there. I still keep in touch with one of them. Judy is a god send as were so many others. Without the support of the staff, I doubt I could have made it through those years. I mentored myself after some of them. I learned a lot both in and out of class and got some pretty good marks along the way.

After graduation, I didn't know what to do. I couldn't find a job so I moved across the country just for a change. I didn't like what I was becoming and thought a change would be helpful. I think it was too.

It took me two years to get a job. I almost gave up. Most employers just wouldn't give me a chance. I was pretty smart but they just wouldn't let me try. Not long before I got a job, I broke down. I was tired and down to washing clothes in the tub because I didn't have $5 to put in the washing machine. I wasn't enjoying most aspects of my life; I was broke, in debt and couldn't see any way out.

I can look back now and see how I did it. I can see how my thoughts changed. I can understand how I made things happen. And things really did start to happen for me.

Once I got my first real job I proved myself in a big way. I moved onto the next job and a few after that. I kept moving up. The apartments got nicer and nicer until I ended up in a house. Then things leveled off. I was sort of stuck in that life. I knew I could do more; I could be more. I needed to make a difference in other people's lives. The office job wasn't giving me that sense of fulfillment anymore. I didn't like the climate where I was living and I didn't really like the house anymore. Most of all, I didn't like working in a job that often left me feeling like a robot and I didn't like the office politics, so I decided that management wasn't for me.

I made pretty good money and I had all the stuff. I was more successful than most of the blind people I knew and had a better life than some of the sighted people I knew. But I wasn't making a difference and I didn't want to die only sort of happy or perhaps moderately satisfied would be a better description. I sure didn't want to look back on my life as not making an impact.

I was living month to month and had no money to take vacations to places I wanted to go. I couldn't see an end to it. Go to work, come home and go to bed, just to do it all again the next day. Look forward to the weekend to do what?

I was in my forties. Frankly I was tired. I'd had enough of being kicked around by life and I had a new disability. My hands were damaged from using the screen reading software at work. Certain key commands that I had to use thousands of times a day just simply wore out my hands. I knew it was only a matter of time before I had to stop working. Ok, that was the last straw!

I started making plans for my own demise … I would take one more shot and if that didn't work, I would just end it all. I couldn't take anymore. I couldn't go back to living in poverty; I was too old and had won too many battles to end up like that again. My hands hurt too much to do laundry in machines now much less kneeling before the tub.

Then I began reviewing all the information that I had purchased over the years. I also took the time to sit back and think about all the people I had met in my life, those I mentored with and those that shared their important wisdom with me.

I had heard all my life that I was a role model. The seeing world had told me over and over. You are amazing. How do you do this or that? I was just doing what I needed to do. I didn't feel too amazing. Not at all!

I dove into the information in a very big way. I thought about it, I lived it and I finally got it. I finally figured out how to implement what I had learned. It wasn't in any one program, book or something someone once said to me. It was there in bits and pieces throughout everything I had learned and I had to pull it all together.

Some people may call the contents of this book secrets. I just call it information. The people who know this information are the wealthiest people in the world; the most successful athletes; the famous musicians; the movie and TV stars; the famous authors etc. In short, the most successful people in the world know this information and they act on it.

Here's the interesting thing. Although all the successful people know this information, they can't necessarily explain it. They just somehow figured it out. Others were taught this information. They are very conscious of how to apply what they know to make whatever they want happen in their lives.

Here's what I mean. I went to a school for the blind from grade 5 on. I know of some young kids who could play the piano better than many adults. One kid I am recalling was only in grade 2 or 3. He was very young and he wasn't taught to play the piano, he just figured it out. Still other blind people I knew took lessons at that school and became brilliant musicians.

If you were to ask that young child now as an adult, how did you get to play the piano so well? He would likely respond with something like, "Oh, I don't know, I loved the piano, I couldn't keep my hands off it, I just figured it out." Now if you were to ask the one that took lessons for years, how did you learn the piano I think the response is pretty obvious. Well, I took lessons and had a great teacher; I worked hard and practiced a lot; I was obsessed about learning it. The end result is the same. Both of those people are very good musicians today.

I would like to stop here for a moment and explain. When I say wealthy or success, I am not just referring to wealth in the sense of money. I am talking about wealth in many ways. Wealth in the family we have, our health, in all aspects of our lives and just being happy all the time. Perhaps another word we could use in place of wealth is abundant.

Here is the bad news. Those of us who don't know this information and have not yet figured it out on our own will not succeed. We will have those unfulfilled dreams. We will live the life of mediocrity at best and poverty at worst. We are the folks who will slave away at a job we don't really like that pays a certain amount week after week, month after month for years. Just having enough money to pay the bills and maybe having some left over to do something nice once in a while. We are the people who are not very happy with our lives. We head home after a day at work and have dinner and maybe watch TV and go to bed after a while just to get up and do it all again. I understand this perfectly, I was one of these people.

It's true. I learned how to break the patterns of that old life and how to create what I wanted. I began reading books and bought many online programs. They all promised to change my life forever. I really don't want to list the books or programs as I don't like to knock someone else's work. I found that although many of these people were no doubt well-meaning, they didn't really give me what I needed to move ahead.

So I spent hundreds and probably even thousands of dollars and didn't really make a lot of progress. Then I decided that I would go back through the information I already had and try various things that they suggested. I would mix things up and find what really works, and when I found what really works, I would write it down and teach others.

Before I could teach anybody anything, I learned something that I will teach you in **Key 1. Who do I listen to?** Ok, so I had the knowledge but I hadn't really attracted anything tangible. I knew I had the power but I couldn't really point at anything and say, look here is what I created. So, I decided that yes I want to teach this to the world and make a difference but I can't stand there with my bare face hanging out and teach this until I created something. Well soon enough I did and the more consistent I became with applying the 4 Keys, the more dreams I fulfilled. Now that my integrity is satisfied, I can teach it to you.

I will share more things as we go through this journey together but here are a few things I attracted. I have a new love and we are a very good match in all ways. I've lived in a beautiful place that overlooks the ocean where I drank my morning tea and listen to the waves roll in. I am not in the nasty winter weather anymore.

I've taken little vacations and bigger ones too. On one vacation, I got to play with a dolphin. I always wanted to do that. I could go on and on but the point is this I am not bragging just telling you that my life changed in huge ways in the fastest time you could imagine.

I recently received an email from one of my students. BJ told me that her first book was just completed and is going to be up for sale in a few days. She thanked me for all of my love and support. She told me that she is a happier person. She is fulfilling her dreams. I am so very proud of her. Now that she has made one dream come true, she knows how to make them all come true.

I have another student who I am working with as I write this book. PG has had it pretty rough. His previous marital relationship was nasty to say the least. He has many musical talents but never really excelled at anything. He had so much to learn and stuck it out. He was willing to change the way he thought and so on. He is now seeing changes in

CHAPTER 3

Our Beliefs

In the coming chapters, I am going to share with you everything that you will ever need to know so you too can dream, believe and achieve anything you want. I have tremendous enthusiasm for the information I am about to share. There are two main reasons for this:

1. It works! Yes, it's that simple. It worked for me and it will work for you. There is no other choice; it has to work for you. I am certain that you will see why it has to work for you as you learn and apply the information.
2. I make a difference! I am so fortunate that I took the time to master this information so that I can teach you. In improving your life, I have made a difference. It's the truth. Think about this. When I make a difference in your life, you will in turn make a difference in those lives around you. What finer purpose can I have than that?

Let's talk about you for a moment. I am reasonably certain that something I say below will ring true to you in some way. I think that much of this is felt in societies all over the world. In fact, when I visited Bali in early 2014, I made some friends there. They live a 5 hour flight away from where I was living at that time but in a totally different world then I am accustomed to.

Their primary religion is Hindu and they don't have much in the way of material things. Their homes are nothing what I would want at any time in my life. They don't even have flush toilets. Since some work in the tourist resorts, they know how different things can be and they surely know about flush toilets. They have plumbing in their homes and I don't know how much it would cost for them to have flush toilets installed but apparently it isn't really a concern for them. Or, they simply have to worry more about putting food on the table and paying for other things that it just isn't a priority. Most of these people drive around on scooters. Me and my buddy Ketut just barely fit on his.

We were talking about buying a home there. I said to Ketut who drives us around, if we move here and I bought a big Harley Davidson motorcycle, how would you like to take your wife for a ride on that? His response was interesting to me. He said no.

The primary reason is that he didn't want to appear rich to those in his village. Of course, I had heard these types of responses from many people I worked with.

This is a block that I've worked on with a number of clients using the Emotional Freedom Technique 'tapping' process.

You might think or feel that I don't want to be rich because my friends and family won't like me anymore. This wonderful lovely man is not just worried about a few people in his life but his whole village.

Do you hold such beliefs? Do you think that you can't be something because of what someone else thinks?

There are also lots of folks who believe they are not smart enough to achieve what they want. Sadly some people are told this as kids growing up. It isn't true, not at all!

Do you think you are not attractive enough? Again this is just silly. If you think for one second that this will stop you from being successful, I suggest you take a look around at some people who are successful.

You know there are performers out there who are brilliant and not very good looking. I bet you have seen some couples where one is very good looking and the other not so much. You see this just isn't a factor and attractive versus not attractive is only something we are taught through images in the media. Beauty truly is in the heart and the eye of the beholder!

There are many reasons why we don't have what we want. I bet that all these reasons really just aren't valid at all. Most of them are other people's beliefs that somewhere along the line got dumped on you.

Let me tell you a bit about you. Obviously, you can read because you made it this far in the book. You are very special because you know that you want to change things in your life. You are reading this book because you know that you need some information to teach you how to change your life. You already have belief that you can change your life. If you didn't you would never have taken the first step to getting this book and you certainly wouldn't have read this far.

So despite your current situation, you are going to succeed. I say this because you have some level of belief in yourself. This is the absolute truth. If you didn't have any belief in yourself, you wouldn't have reached out. What would be the point, right?

Now then, you hang on to that belief, even if it is only a weak thin shred of belief. Hang on to it. Nurture it. Just know that you will soon be making things happen. Hug that belief and this book to your heart.

I did believe it. I just knew I could do something amazing with my life. I didn't care that I am blind. So I can't hear everything. I have trouble sometimes with the simplest of tasks because I can't see. My hands hurt so much it took me months instead of days to write this book. It just didn't matter. No one can take away my belief and knowledge.

I always had people who thought I wouldn't make anything out of my life. Some of these people were teachers of the blind. That's right, they were responsible for teaching blind people and yet they thought I would not do anything of value with my life. It's easy to understand a 'normal' person looking at me and feeling pity for me and thinking that I could never amount to anything. It amuses me that lots of people who spent so much time with blind people would have this opinion of me or any blind person for that matter.

You see my point? It just doesn't matter what others think. It only matters what you think and believe. So, you just hang on to that belief in yourself you have right now. I swear, you will be amazing. I really am excited for you and I am so grateful that you chose me as your teacher or mentor.

Before We Get Started

Here are some things I would like you to do and understand before you start the learning process:

1. Get a pen with blue ink and a notepad. Do not take notes on the computer. There is magic in the written word. Just trust me on this.

2. In that notebook, I want you to write down the date you started this learning process. I want you to write down the date you finished reading this book the first time. Then do it again. Every time you go through this book, write down the start and end dates.

   Now, every time you read something that jumps out at you write it down. This is very important to your success.

3. Take that blue pen and white paper and write down everything you want. It doesn't matter right now if it is big or small. Just write them all down. You can categorize them if you want.

   How you want your health to be?

   How you look and feel?

   How much money you have?

   Your loving relationship.

   Family relationships.

   The kind of friends you have.

   The house you live in.

   Vacations you take.

The car you drive.

The career you enjoy.

Just write down everything and anything you want. Have fun with this process.

4. While learning the information in this book, do not read any other book. Don't listen to other presenters. Just focus on this book. I can't stress enough the importance of mastering what I teach without confusing yourself by listening to others.
5. Block time every day to read this book. Put it on your calendar. Do whatever it takes to not be distracted during this time. Shut off Facebook, turn off the phone, no texting or emails.
6. When you are given an action to take in this book, do it. Sounds simple right? Just do it! Get the results you want and deserve.
7. Don't ever get stuck. If something doesn't quite ring right with you, don't worry. The next time you go through this book and the time after that, you will find that things become clearer. You see you are starting someplace. Right now something will jump out at you and make total sense. Something may not. It's a learning process. Give yourself a chance to learn new concepts and ideas. Just move on and never get stuck.

Please don't jump ahead and skip chapters. I took a great deal of time to lay out the information in the most logical way I know. It is best that you learn the information in the order presented. I will pull it all together for you so have no concerns at all.

Here is some of the information in this book.

4 Keys

The 4 keys are not just things that are nice to know, they need to be applied all the time to make sure you are on the right track. They are vital and will most definitely separate those who will succeed from those who will not. I simply can't stress this enough!

Recently, I was talking to someone I just met. The gent asked me what I do for work. I explained that I teach people how to be successful and to make it possible for people to dream, believe and achieve whatever they want. So we talked a bit. I explained that I started with the 4 keys. He said what are they? As I was saying them he kept saying "yeah, I've heard something like that before," and other such mouth noises. He just brushed them off. I knew that he invested other people's money for a living. Maybe that is his dream, I don't know. Let's assume it's not.

He had heard about something like my 4 keys. I know he's not applying them. I could feel it. I kind of felt sad for him.

We always need to learn. We grow or we die. Please don't let this happen to you. Learn them, master them and be great!

Fears and Actions

We all have fears and it is those fears that will often stop us cold. I had them. I was stopped many times. You can get beyond the fears and you can take action and in doing so you will succeed.

Do you know that today there really isn't all that much to fear at a basic level? We are human. We don't have a lot of bigger animals chasing us around so we can be their dinner. Most of us really don't need to worry about the basic needs in life. Yes, I am aware that there are many people, too many people that do. I plan to help them in my own, shall we say, quiet way. We can't sit back and let government take all the responsibility. Yes, this is one of my dreams that I will manifest.

I believe that in most cases all we fear is the unknown. We listen to the people who think small and safe. How can you start a business? How can you leave that job for a better one? What about security and on and on. I've heard all this stuff directly said to me. Remember I can't see or hear that well either. Did I have fears? Sure, at one time I really did. I think you will find this section helpful. So don't worry or be fearful about this. I will share with you various things that you can do to eliminate fear.

Law of Attraction

In order to be successful in this process, it is helpful to have a basic understanding of the Law of Attraction (LOA); how it can help you and how best to apply the techniques to make your dreams come true.

I don't go into a lot of depth in this area. I just don't think you need to know more than the basics. If you want to learn more perhaps I will write more about it someday.

Keep this in mind. You are how old? You realistically have how much time left? My responsibility is to give you the information you require to make your dreams become a reality. I never forget that this is your goal. To this end, I will focus your thoughts to the important information you need to achieve.

Feeling Good Now

If you go through your day feeling angry or sad or have any negative feelings at all, this too will block you from success. This is crucial information for you to have.

You can see it in other people's faces as you go through your day. Pay attention to how you feel. Are you happy most of the time or do you walk around like a defeated person?

I know, life can be hard a lot of the time. Did you know there are some very simple things you can do to feel better right this very second? Just smile a huge smile. Do it right now. You feel better now than you just did a few seconds ago right?

Gratitude

Being grateful throughout the day will help you increase your power to attract things. This will also help you feel good.

Try this the next time you are at a store. Don't just say an off-handed thanks to the person at the checkout. Smile and give them a more enthusiastic thank you. Do this everywhere you go. It may not make everyone feel better but I am confident that you will make some people feel happier. You will see it in their return smile or maybe their eyes will light up just a little more.

You know one thing I doubt most of us do. We don't thank the people around us nearly enough. We are pretty good at thanking strangers but not the people closest to us.

Try gratitude and don't take things for granted.

The Power of Belief

You must believe to achieve. If you don't believe that you can achieve something then there isn't anything I can do to help you.

Don't worry if you have little belief now, your belief will increase as you go through this program. As you learn the correct techniques and realize just how simple the process is, your belief will go higher and higher.

Three Methods to Attract

Specific, general, or just feeling good! When should you use which method?

There are some things you will want to be very specific about. Other things you should be very general about. There are still other times when just feeling good will bring you what you want.

In most cases, being general will usually result in you getting something even better than if you are so specific. This is half the fun.

Visualize/Intention

How to stay focused on what you want. There are tips and tricks for helping you to remain focused for long enough periods to make a difference in your life.

This is an absolutely enjoyable process. Doing this will result in many good things. You will feel great and it will help you to make things happen faster. Sometimes faster than you could ever imagine.

The Simple Procedure

Please don't skip to this section. It pulls together everything you have learned so far in this book. And provides a step by step guide on how to make your dreams come true. This is what the whole program is designed to do, to make your dreams come true.

Play with this Information

You may have read other books or programs that told you to dream big. Make those dreams huge. There are problems with this when you are just starting out. I believe that this will destroy your success.

I am not saying that you can't make the big dreams come true. Of course you can. I am saying that you need to build your confidence by attracting some smaller things first.

By the way, did you know that there is really no such thing as small or large? It's true. It all depends on your belief. You can attract something smaller like $10 or something larger such as a million bucks. This is all part of the learning process. Enjoy that process.

Tips

The healthier you are, the more power you can put out. The cleaner the body, the clearer the mind.

More Information

In this section, I will answer some of the more common questions. Various situations are explained which will provide you with more information to help you.

More on Thoughts

This chapter talks about the 2%, 3% and 95% rule on thinking. Do you actually think or do you just react? Hmm …

A Bit About Money

Some things that will help you to earn more money if that is your goal.

EFT or Tapping

What is this and what is it good for? How can you learn more about it.

Some thoughts about the learning process. Learning is very much an individual process for each person. One person may be able to sit down for an hour and read a lot of this book and retain what they have learned. Others need to take it slower. One is not better than the other. I suggest that you read one chapter at a time. Take the time to make notes about it and how you are going to apply the knowledge. If you read something and don't do anything with the information you have just learned it won't get you the success you desire.

No matter what, do not get overwhelmed. Don't worry about how you are going to learn the information. I will explain things for you. The key is if something doesn't quite ring true to you right now is to just dive in and take action. It is the very act of doing something that will help you. If you don't take action, I can guarantee that you will not get the success that you want and deserve.

Trust the process and have fun with it.

Dream, believe and achieve whatever you want.

CHAPTER 4

The 4 Keys

The 4 keys are not just basic information that can be glanced over. These are Keys; they will guide you and keep you focused. You must know them intimately and apply them in your life every day. You have to focus on them all day long. These Keys are not taught by many people, and well, they should be learned. Trust me for now and learn them. As the program unfolds you will see more and more about how they impact you.

Key #1

Who Should I Listen To?

There are a lot of well-meaning people in the world who believe they have information that is valuable. However, there is also a lot of misinformation floating around which keeps people thinking they are learning the gold but it's not quite enough to be very successful. They will then claim that it is your fault for not following your passions and dreams. Or worse, you get some success but not enough to improve your life in a meaningful way. I think this is sad!

You need to listen to those who have proven what they are teaching. Remember also that books authored by some rich famous people may not have been written by that person. They often have a ghost writer and just answer questions but the information is stated as though they have written the book. You can see quickly how this can lead to a great deal of misinformation.

There are, of course, some famous people who have written every word in their book. The point I am making is, be aware that the information you read may not be coming from the author themselves.

I personally decided a long time ago that once I got results I would then be able to teach this information. I did have the knowledge for some years, however I wasn't applying it all the time and therefore only got some results. I have since learned to apply it consistently and have manifested fantastic results. Not only that but I have tested these practices with others who have also manifested results. Now I feel my ethics are satisfied and I can help you dream, believe and achieve whatever you want.

I did not create this information. I merely pulled it together from a wide range of sources to provide you with a complete process. This information has been around since the beginning of time and is reflected in such books as the bible, other religious books, and it is stated that this information is known as well as protected by various secret and not so secret organisations. I don't know if this is true as I am not a member. Would it surprise me to learn this is indeed the truth? Not at all.

At one time I had a life that many would find to be reasonably successful. I had a good enough job. I didn't like my job much but it paid the bills most of the time. Since applying what I have learned, I have lived in beautiful homes overlooking the ocean. I can sit outside and listen to the waves roll in. I have a beautiful new lady who I adore and who loves me right back. I eat the best foods and drink finer wines when I want, and I live in a wonderful climate. So can you listen to me? I think you can.

Who do you listen to? Listen to those who have what you want or have the evidence that what they are telling you is true.

When I learned all the information I am presenting to you, I started reading some biographies and autobiographies of the people I admired. The interesting thing I found while reading those books is:

- I could see clearly what they did to be successful even though it wasn't stated in so many words.

- I could also identify what they did wrong when they had tough times.

You will be able to do this too when you master everything in this book. If you want to be a great musician then read books about great musicians. If you want to be a great teacher then learn about the great teachers including those who came before us.

Again, don't read about these people until you have gone through this program completely many times. First get the right knowledge so you don't learn incomplete or incorrect information.

Getting the correct knowledge first is vital. In everything we learn, we can pick up the bad habits of those we are learning from. If you are old enough, you probably learned how to drive a car from your parents. Many people today take driving lessons so they can learn all the good habits and how to drive safely.

If I want to learn how to cook a gourmet meal I'm not going to ask a short order cook to teach me. I'm going to research gourmet chefs until I find the one who prepares the meals I want to create. Then I would mentor myself after that person.

If you want to be a musician or a classical singer then you don't want to learn how to sing from a country singer. Frankly I prefer new country but I digress.

If you want to be wealthy then study those who have the kind of wealth you want. Don't study from a poor man.

Think of yourself as a mentee. Choose your mentors carefully and be like them. Act the way they do. Talk like they do. Adopt their habits and observe the way they interact with you and other people. See the way he/she responds to others and how others respond to them.

Who should I listen to? You listen to those who have what you want or can teach you how to get it.

Who don't you listen to? Don't listen to those who don't have a clue what they are talking about and have no evidence of what they say is true.

All of these keys are very complex. Their meanings will change from day to day as you face various situations. However, the simplest way to remember this key is:

Who do I listen to? I listen to those who have what I want.

Key #2

Am I Teachable?

You obviously need to be teachable. If you are not teachable then nothing I can share with you will work. Don't worry if you are not so sure right now just how teachable you are. Maybe you are very sceptical. That's fine. You will become more and more teachable throughout the process.

There are two sides to Am I Teachable?

1. Am I willing to accept change?
2. What am I willing to give up to learn this information?

So, 'Am I willing to accept change?' Are you willing to change the way you think about things, the way you feel? This may be quite obvious but think of it like this. If you continue to think the way you've always thought, then you will continue to get what you've always got.

But, I wasn't taught to think that way? That's right you probably weren't. This is why you will need to change the way you think about things. You need to be a perfect 10 on this and have a high willingness to accept change. This will go down from time to time. And that's why it is so important to keep it at the front of your mind.

The reason that it will go down from time to time is simply because you have learned all you can at that time. It doesn't mean you are not going to learn more; it just means that you need to take a break before you are ready to move on. I will state this several times - You can't just read this program once and get it all. No one can. You need to read this program over and over until you master all the information I have to teach you. Be a master yourself.

Also, if I say something you don't believe or think is correct then go back to the keys. You will see that your willingness to accept change is low. I hope you are beginning to see why these are keys and not just nice things to know.

One student I was working with was telling me that he found himself slipping back into the old patterns of thinking. He was finding that he wasn't feeling as good and started listing the bad things happening to him. That is when this key really made its way into his life. He learned that he had to change his thoughts and the way he felt about things. He needed to keep his mind on being willing to change.

Some people will need to change the way they eat, walk, talk, dress and in short everything about themselves. When you mentor after someone who is successful then you really want to take on as many traits of that person as you can. Again, don't worry, this will become more clear to you as you go through the information.

What Am I Willing To Give Up To Learn This Information? You must be willing to give up things you love; time, money, hobbies and so on. If you don't give up something then you simply won't get through the program once much less learn anything.

Did I mention that sometimes my words may appear harsh? If so I apologise. I will hammer a point hard to get you to understand something. So please don't take anything I say the wrong way.

If you are one of the many who say, "Yes, I would love to learn this stuff and make things happen but I've got to read emails or jump on Facebook or watch my show on TV" you are not going to be one of the few who learn and master this information. So, bottom line in this section is you have to give up your time. You already gave up some money to get this program.

Be aware of time wasters. These are the things that take up your time and don't give you any benefits. How about this: You come home from work, have dinner and think well I will just sit down and watch TV for a few minutes and read Michael's book. Next thing you know you look at the clock and it's time for bed. Your eyes never once diverted from the all mighty TV or the computer screen. You didn't even open the book. What a waste of time. This applies to all the different time wasters like Facebook, texting, gaming, emails and so on.

In college I learned about time management. Over the years, I have come to realize that it isn't at all what we should be focusing on. It's all about priority management. Simply put, write down what your highest priorities are for that day. Be sure to have learning this program in there. Schedule it in and don't let anything stop you from keeping this appointment today for your future.

So you must be a perfect 10 in your willingness to accept change and a perfect 10 in your willingness to give up something to learn this information. If you are a 10 times 10 (100), then you are the perfect student. You will be the one who makes a difference, not only in your life but in the lives of others as well.

Just so you know. I doubt that anyone can be a perfect 100 point student all the time. There's nothing wrong with that. It just means that you need to focus on this all the time. It may be that you have learned all you can for that moment. Never worry about this as you are going to go through the program many times. Just make sure that you focus on being teachable as far as being willing to accept change and willing to give up your time and money to learn this life changing information.

Key #3

Where Do I Focus My Thoughts?

There are two sides to this; the how and the thoughts.

You have probably been taught to place your focus on the how. Most of us have. We are taught this in schools and from our parents and grandparents and even our friends. How are you going to have more money? How are you going to get that new car. How can you have your own business? On and on.

Here are some more words for the how: process, analyze, techniques, plans, activities, figure out and so on. These are the action steps.

Here are some words for the thoughts side: wish, dreams, thinking and thoughts.

So the thoughts side is when you are thinking about an old friend you haven't talked to in a while. The how or actions side is when you get on the computer and contact your friend or pick up the phone and call.

I went to Business College and mainly studied management studies. One of the courses I took was how to open and run a small business. They showed me all the ways that opening a small business wouldn't work. All the 'hows' were too much; the market research and choosing a location, what products to sell, how that product will make money and so on. It was really crazy. Of course, the old kick in the head that over 90% of small businesses fail in their first five years.

Ok, so how can I open a business and be successful when I have all this against me? Here's the big point. We have been taught to focus our thoughts on the how side; the actions steps. You must know how you are going to make something work. I am here to tell you that this is the wrong way to think. You must always focus your thoughts on the dream, the want, the desire. Yes, this is a different way to think about things. Remember, am I teachable right now? If this concept appears to be too hard for you, what is your willingness to accept change? I hope you are beginning to understand why these keys are not just basic information. They really are the keys.

Back in my college days, I was talking to a friend of mine. CP wanted to make hockey sticks. He was a pretty smart guy. I can remember clearly his excitement about this venture. I said let's play devil's advocate for a bit. I then started asking all the stuff that I had learned in college. I am sad to say that soon his mood dropped and he said, "I thought you would have supported me." Man, what an idiot I was then.

If CP came to me today I would handle it completely differently. I would get excited with him and explore why his sticks would be different or whatever his plans were. The how would sort itself out. I would have gotten in his dream just like I do my own dreams now. Just like I do with anyone I talk to or coach.

You will learn later why the how is not important and in fact will stop you cold. For now it is enough to drive this point into your head and hold it there. You must place 99.9% of your thoughts on the dream.

Key #4

How do I learn?

These are the four steps to learning. Very useful information as you can use this to help you identify where you are in learning anything. I will list them and then explain.

1. Unconscious incompetence
2. Conscious incompetence

3. Conscious competence
4. Unconscious competence

1. Unconscious Incompetence. This is simply when you don't even know that you don't know something. Think back to when you were a baby. There was a time when you didn't even know that you didn't know how to spell your name.
2. Conscious incompetence. This is when you did learn that you didn't know how to spell your name. You now know that you don't know how to spell your name.
3. Conscious competence. You now know how to spell your name but you have to think it through. It is a process at this step.
4. Unconscious competence. You spell your name without having to think about it. You know with no effort. This is when the magic happens. It is a part of you.

Have you ever driven to work and wondered how you even got there? You don't remember the trip at all? It's because driving to work is simply part of you. There was a time when you had to learn the way. You maybe even took a wrong turn or two back in the beginning. Now you just go there like the car is driving itself. You are on automatic pilot; you are using unconscious competence.

Think about this the next time you tie your shoe laces. You know there was a time when you didn't even know how to tie your shoe laces. Of course there was. Then you grew a little older and you were running around and your shoe lace came undone. All of a sudden you realized that you didn't know how to tie it back up. Where's mom or dad?

Someone showed you how to tie your shoe laces. Then you had to think the process through. Make the rabbit ear, wrap the lace around and so on. Before long you were able to tie your very own shoe laces all by yourself.

Now you just bend down and like magic, the shoe is tied and just the way you like it too. Not too tight and not too loose.

You will learn in this program how to make things happen at this fourth step. A lot of people get stuck on Step 3. I believe this happens because they start to make their dreams come true and they get satisfied there. Well I am here to tell you that those who get to the fourth step are those who can really make the magic happen. Yes, you can do just that. They make dreams come true without ever thinking about it. These are the people who live a life of joy and excitement all the time.

You must master the **4 Keys** and make them your own. Apply them to your situation in that moment. They will pop up all day long in your everyday life. Who do I listen to? You're having a chat with a friend and they say something you know is wrong. You will stop for a split second and say, who do I listen to? Does he or she have what I want? You find yourself slipping into your old ways of thinking about something. How teachable am I? Am I willing to change the way I think? Am I willing to give up watching that TV show to learn? Where should I focus my thoughts? Do I focus on how I will do something or just think about that something? Where am I in the four steps? Do I know the information at the highest level?

These keys will guide you in ways you may not understand right now. They will keep you on track.

I suggest you take that blue pen and white paper and write these 4 Keys out every single day until you know, know, know them. Also be sure to state what they mean to you in that moment. Give a little example of how it popped up for you during that day.

My students who have done this exercise are the ones who have made the quickest progress.

One lady I worked with didn't really give learning the keys a high priority. During one of our lessons she was telling me something about what someone else said. It was bad information. I stopped her and said "Key #1." The light went on. Oh she knew the keys and could give them back to me but she just wasn't applying them. So I made a point of stating key numbers as we talked. She told me she was very grateful I did that. Then she was able to see just how often they do come up in her day and just how important they really are.

I very much encourage you to take the time right now to write the 4 Keys out. Don't be one of those who doesn't listen to me. Who do you listen to? Well then do it. Don't move on in this wonderful learning process until you have begun to learn these keys.

Dream, believe and achieve whatever you want.

CHAPTER 5

Fears Defeat and Action

Did you know that very often there is only one thing that stops us from dreaming, believing, and achieving what we want? It can be summed up in this one word: Fear! We fear failure or success because you may fear losing what you have right now. Or you may fear anything to do with change. This is part of Key 2 right? You need to be open to changing the way you think and behave.

If we take a look at where a lot of fears come from it may help in removing them. Often the fears we have are from other people's sayings, thoughts and beliefs. They are not even our own. They often aren't. They are other people's beliefs. Think about that for a moment. Are you going to let something that someone said all those years ago control you now? I sure hope not.

Gary Craig, the grandfather of Emotional Freedom Technique explains this well. He calls it the writing on our wall. Things that people said become the writing on our wall. Our beliefs. Grandma told our mom something then our mom tells us. It must be correct because it is passed down from generation to generation.

An example: If mom is afraid of dogs, she flinches every time a dog comes near. We see this when we are young. If we never meet a nice dog then we may react with this fear. This fear becomes the writing on our wall.

There are also down right harmful things that are said to us. Things said in anger or someone just being mean. For some reason we take what was said and it appears on our wall. This wall can be filled with a lot of junk that isn't helpful in our lives at all. So just be aware of the writing on your wall and be willing to erase it and replace it with good and useful information. Information from Key #1. Who do I listen to?

I am blind right? I can't see my hand in front of my own face. I haven't seen me since I was nine or ten years old. Others looked at me and felt sorry for me. They hinted or said that my brother will be the one to succeed. Michael can't! How will a blind man do well?

I had some teachers at the school for the blind who said you aren't going to make it. I bet that I was the one near the bottom of the list of those who would make a difference and succeed.

I met some of those teachers after I had this so called good job and a respectable life. They were surprised. Those who figured I would become successful said how proud they were of me. They knew I would do well.

Now did I have fears? You better believe I did. That's why I took the jobs I did. That's why I settled for that house I did. Because somewhere along the way I picked up on what others were saying. I couldn't be anything more than a good employee and so on. That mental wall of mine had some limiting things written on it.

What did I fear? Well one thing is that I did have a good enough job. If I stopped working I could never get a job that paid that much if I failed. I had to go through a long time over two years just to get my first job. It was hard for a blind person to get a chance. Have things changed? Well no, at least not if I thought now the way I did then. But, let's just stay with the mainstream thinking for a moment. It is very hard for a person to get a decent paying job. So it's next to impossible for a blind person who can't hear all that well. These are the so called facts.

My little rant on facts … I believe that facts are nothing more than someone else's opinion. The fact is that the economy may be very bad right now, then why is it that during the great depression a lot of millionaires were created?

In modern times, why is it that some businesses are going down while others are growing?

Good old fear. Sorry but I think that the so called F word isn't the one you are thinking. I think the F word stands for fear. It is fear that has killed so many people's dreams. Fear is the reason that we are in a relationship that doesn't satisfy most of our needs. Fear locks us down and keeps us there in so many ways.

Here is a thought. What is the opposite of fear? I think the answer is love. So live a life of love and not fear. How nice is that!

I was in church one day. The minister was talking about love. He explained what love was, well sort of. He said that there are many kinds of love. There is how you love your parents, how you love your mate, how you love chocolate or your pets. You can learn to love everything that you do. Yes, even the mundane daily chores. You may not ever love doing the dishes but you sure can love it when everything is clean and put away.

Perhaps another form of love is pride. If you take pride in everything that you do won't that make you feel good?

Here is a thought of how some people lose everything. You've probably read stories about a celebrity who was wealthy and then broke? I bet they were living in fear of losing it all. So they lost it all. So fears can and will change as we change. It's very interesting this fear conspiracy.

I don't fear losing it all. I have lost everything. It's not that bad. I built a life and lost it. Not a big deal. I build something stronger and better just by using the techniques you are learning in this book. It is really quite fun to see how things will work out. Frankly I enjoy the process.

I suggest you stop now and write down as many fears as you can that you experience. All the fears that are stopping you cold. Fears that you have learned from others. Fears that lurk in the back of your mind. Just write them all down. Perhaps:

Fear of being wealthy
Fear of failing
Fear of the economy
Fear that I'm not smart enough
Fear of losing friends or family

Fear of losing what I have

Now that you have that list, look it over and see how many of them are actual fears. Are they things that you should really fear? As humans we don't really have to fear for our lives, we don't have big hairy beasts chasing us around to make us their dinner. When you consider fear in a life and death manner, I can guess that most of the fears you have are ones more or less learned. These fears are the ones that you can overcome.

I think simply the act of writing down our fears and reviewing that list, you will see that most of these fears really aren't fears at all. Most of them are simply things that we were told by others. They may warrant some concern, maybe. But they aren't real big ugly beasty fears. Most of these fears you have can be overcome just by taking action.

Perhaps the simplest way to overcome your fears is to just take action. Yes, I know this sounds too simple. We humans just love to complicate issues. We needlessly complicate things. I say so often, "Keep it simple"! Some like the KISS saying, 'Keep It Simple Stupid' but I don't like that very much. How about this, keep it Super Simple"? That sounds so much nicer and no-one needs to feel insulted. Yes, much better.

Many years ago, I remember dad telling me the story about how he learned to swim or at least eliminate his fear of the water. When he was young a swim instructor got little dad to get on the low diving board. Dad walked out to the end of that board. He stood there looking down at the water. All he had to do was jump. Just jump. He was stuck. Too afraid to jump and too afraid to go back. The instructor took a long poll that he would use to rescue someone who was in trouble. He took that poll and knocked my dad in. Well dad swam the whole length of the pool. When he got to the other end, the instructor met him and lifted him out. He hugged my dad and told him how proud of him he was. I am assuming this isn't the method that is used today. It sure worked though. After that, dad was no longer afraid of the water.

My dad was forced into action to get over his fear of the water. He was knocked in to the pool. Bottom line, he got over his fear. Ok, no I don't think that this is the best way to overcome his fear but it did work. I use EFT or tapping to help people get rid of their bigger fears and phobias.

If you are afraid to walk up to someone and ask them something, just don't think about that fear. Know what you want to ask and go to it. Walk up to that person and ask. Gee, I wonder just how many of those girls would have said yes back in those teenage years? Hmm.

Pick up the phone and make that call. Take the action.

During my career in the big offices, I knew I needed some help. I needed to be recognised for the person I was and not just the fact that I am blind. I somehow needed to attract the attention of the upper managers. They didn't really know what I did at my desk all day. That's my immediate supervisor's job not the manager's job.

First I started asking around about this manager and that one. I knew what I wanted to hear. Again, being blind and over half deaf I couldn't just observe like others. I wanted to know who was the most popular manager, not only with the staff but also with the other managers, and one name kept turning up.

Ok, now I knew the 'who' but how can I contact him. Yep good old fear kicked in. In fact it stopped me for a while. I believe it was some weeks before I took action. I decided to keep it simple. I sent him an email. I kept it short and asked him if I could meet with him to discuss my mentoring with him or if he could suggest someone else if he was too busy.

I took action and it was easy. Really, the worst that could have happened is he thought I was a bit of an idiot but how bad could that be? There are other managers.

The end result was that he became my mentor and friend. He helped me in many ways. He helped me with personal development as well as getting me an opportunity at certain jobs. I overcame my fear and it paid off.

Taking action can be so very simple. The problem comes when we get stuck in the fear and are paralyzed. Don't overanalyze something, just take action.

I had an aunt who was out of a job. She was an aunt that I was pretty close to. She was tough as nails. Boy, when she told you to do something, you sure did it. Don't get me wrong she wasn't nasty in any way, just had a tough way about her.

She was telling my mom that she thought she would sell cosmetics. I couldn't believe my ears. My feisty smart funny aunt said, "I couldn't get out of my car to go to the first house." I was too scared. She said she sat there and couldn't do it. The longer she sat, the more stuck she was. So, she didn't do it. She didn't sell anything and that was that for that.

She was paralyzed in Key #3. Where do I place my thoughts? She was thinking about the how. She was worried about being turned away and I just bet her mind was racing down all the hows. If she was thinking only about the dream, she would love to meet new people, providing someone with a great product and having some fun, she probably would have jumped right out of that car and walked straight up to that door.

I bet she would have been pretty good at it. She would have enjoyed meeting people and had lots of fun along the way. She didn't meet one person. All because of fear.

I was young then. It always stuck with me. I somehow figured out what she did so called 'wrong'. She was on the how side and didn't take action. What if she pulled up confident, that she knew her stuff, and simply turned off the car, got out right away and walked up to the first door. No way to know of course but at least she would have been able to give it a shot.

How many girls didn't I ask out because of fear? What's the worst that could have happened? What they'd laugh at me? A girl who is that mean isn't someone I would have wanted to date anyway. Just maybe they would have said yes. All I had to do was take action.

Now, I did take action where others in my situation probably wouldn't. I moved across the country with my then girlfriend. Yes, just packed up a few things and off we went. People around me were trying to put the fears in me. I didn't listen. I just said this is what we decided to do and that's it. Sure there were some hard times but we also had a lot of wonderful experiences there too.

After a couple of years, I finally found a job and worked there for around six months or so and then moved to another job. I didn't even know what the new job really was. I just heard more security and more money. Ok, I'll make that work and I did.

A year or so later, I moved back across the country for another job. Another two or more steps up the ladder and in another city I didn't know. It was fun. It was exciting. I didn't have fear and just dove in and took action.

Don't worry this program is going to teach you how to dream, believe and achieve what you want. You will never have to follow the path I took in those days before I understood this information.

Another word about fear. Sometimes just taking action sounds too simple for some people. Perhaps you may have a fear that is more deeply rooted. Something I have studied will help you. Emotional Freedom Technique (EFT) or simply 'Tapping' is very effective at removing blocks to your success.

I began studying Tapping in 2006. I have since worked with many people and help them in different ways. Fear being an emotion is easily overcome by tapping. You can tap on yourself or connect with a practitioner. I will have more about this later. I am considering designing some programs to help people with many of the more common issues. However, some issues do require a practitioner's assistance. I suggest you stay on my email list or get on it if you aren't currently. You can learn more about that at the end of this book.

The email list is how I will be able to keep you up to date. I will let you know of seminars you will want to attend and other materials I have reviewed and suggest and much more.

So the big thing about fear is really like everything else I teach. Just keep it simple, take action and the fear will disappear in most cases.

Defeat

Do you know that one of the biggest problems today is that so many people walk around with the defeatist attitude? They beat themselves up before they even start? Yes, I am even guilty of this from time to time.

I was listening to an old friend of mine who is a rather famous guitar player. Many have said that he is one of the best in the world. He sure is amazing. I remember thinking something like "I could never play guitar like that."

Ouch, of course I can do anything I want. I changed my thoughts to simply saying, "he's an amazing musician: I can dream, believe and achieve anything I want. I know this. So if I want to be an amazing guitar player then that's what I will become.

Defeat is only something that's in your mind. Think about that. You often hear someone say that they couldn't do something right after they tried. "I knew that I couldn't do it." "I was pretty sure my business would fail."

You are going to learn more about this later but if you think you will fail then you will. This is the defeatist's credo. Those who will never succeed will hold this to their heart until their dying day.

How do you react to defeat? When you experience defeat do you simply give up? I believe that most people do. You've probably heard the stories of many wealthy people who didn't make it the first time. They persevered and eventually they did succeed. Not to worry, of course, the reason you got this program is to learn how to be successful. This you will learn. My point is that many people just simply quit and don't keep trying until they succeed.

If we take a look at me … I am blind and I could have been satisfied just sitting back and collecting a disability pension and remaining on or below the poverty line. I made up my mind that I wouldn't live like that for the rest of my life. Was I defeated? Many times.

I had a job all lined up, things were looking good. So I decided to take my meager savings and go back home to see my friends and family before I started my new job. The lady who was hiring me said that I was going to be employed when I came back. After a nice vacation, I came back to learn that in order to be hired I had to go to another country to be trained for three months by someone who was blind. At that time in my life, there was no way that was going to happen. So another opportunity down the tubes for me and I was even worse off than I was before I so called had that job. I was worse off since I had spent all the money I had in the bank. I'm pretty sure that was when I was washing clothes in the tub. I didn't have enough money to use the laundry machines.

It may have defeated me for a bit. I was so close to just saying to hell with it and go crawling back home to my family. But I just couldn't give up. At least I had a roof over my head and enough money for food. I didn't have money for anything else. So I hung in there. Keeping in mind this was years before I learned how to make things happen. This was many years before I learned what I am teaching you now. So I fought the good fight and things slowly changed for me.

So if defeat is nothing more than self-talk. We can just as easily change that too right? Yes, we can. The great inventors didn't invent something on their first try. They kept trying. They must have had the thought of "Ok, that didn't work, so let's try this."

They learned how to overcome their little defeats and turn them into successes. It has been stated that Edison when inventing the incandescent light bulb said that he successfully found 999 ways that it didn't work. What a great way to think about it. We can always learn something from not only our successes but also our so called failures.

The most important thing to remember is that you can simply forget about your past and only live in the present. Did you know there is no past or future? There is only now. If this statement doesn't currently make sense, it will as you learn more. Fear can usually be overcome through action. The defeatist attitude can be overcome by changing your thoughts to being positive and in some cases learning from what happened previously.

Now let's move on so I can teach you how to avoid all this negative stuff from ever happening to you or ever happening to you again.

Dream, believe and achieve whatever you want.

CHAPTER 6

Law of Attraction

While it is helpful for you to know about the Law of Attraction (LOA), I don't go into a lot of detail as I simply don't believe you need to understand it at a deep level. However, I believe that if you do have a basic understanding, it will assist you in moving forward at a faster rate.

If this is the first book or program that you have studied about LOA fear not. Some people may find this a bit of a stretch for their current belief structure. This is back to Key #2: Am I willing to accept change? Are you willing to change the way you think to make a difference in your life? Remember, if you continue to think what you've always thought then you will continue to get what you've always got. This just simply makes sense. You are with me to make a difference in some manner to your life. So be aware that you need to change the way you think about things and be willing to accept new ideas in order to change things in your life.

I remember when I first started to learn about LOA. Frankly I wasn't so sure that I needed this information. The way some folks explained it was just too out there for me to swallow. Others explained it in such a complicated way that I didn't understand. Then when I finally started to get it, I decided that yes this information is necessary to understand. However, I don't think it needs to be broken down into too much detail.

I will first explain what LOA is and some detail about it. Then, I will explain why it is important to get an understanding of it and keep that in your mind. Stay with me and always continue to honour your learning process.

What is Law of Attraction?

LOA is the big boy of all laws. It is the master. Think about the law of gravity. What goes up must come down. Have you heard about the gardener's law? That states what goes down must come up. Ok, I digress.

The law of gravity is simply this. You toss something up and it comes down. That is a law that I think we can all understand and agree with. Is the law of gravity the highest law? The answer is no. There is also the law of lift. It is the law of lift that allows birds to fly and those massive large airplanes to soar about the clouds.

So one can say that the law of gravity, although being a law isn't a big boy of the laws. There is nothing that supersedes LOA. It is the biggest of the big boys. Now allow me to explain about LOA.

The simple rule of LOA is this. What you think and feel is what you get back. I will say this again. What you think, and feel, you get back.

Do you know someone who is miserable all the time? They walk around with a growl on their face. Bad stuff seems to happen to that person over and over. Maybe that's you? Flip the coin. How about knowing someone who is successful? That person walks around happy and enjoys life. They are the so called lucky ones. Everything works out for them. The miserable person is saying, "If I didn't have bad luck, I wouldn't have any luck at all." Wow, isn't that just nasty stuff. Here is what's going on.

None of this information is new. I didn't invent it. I just learned how to use it. Thomas Edison and Albert Einstein stated it way back then. Thoughts are real things. They said it; thoughts are particles that go out there. How amazing is that! Ok, you aren't overly excited yet.

Depending on your age you were taught that the smallest thing is the atom. Everything is made up of atoms. Your hand, the desk, the food you eat, the pretty flowers, your clothes. Everything is made up of atoms. There is nothing smaller than the atom. Well because it was proven then that the smallest thing was an atom, that doesn't mean the smallest thing is the atom.

We later learned that an electron travels around the atom. Here's the kicker, we couldn't see what held the electron there. Well my friend that is energy. Ok, still not excited? Let's keep going.

Energy, or vibration, or frequency, is smaller than the smallest thing we know of. This is why cell phones can work in many cases through walls and most other matter. The energy travels through most things because it is smaller than the smallest thing, atoms. Are you starting to get a little excited yet?

Try this on. Your thoughts are particles that are put out as energy. Your thoughts go out there. This energy, unlike cell towers, doesn't just go out in a single direction. Your brain puts out energy at a very powerful rate in all directions. Yes, your brain is the most powerful sender and receiver of information there is. Now that's very cool.

Edison and Einstein knew this way back then. Others knew this information as well. Some say that it was kept from the masses on purpose. I mentioned about perhaps there was a conspiracy to keep this information quiet. I don't know if that's true or not. I can see why they would want it quiet though because they need the masses to work or who will do the jobs? Not me, not anymore. I am going to teach everything I know to anyone who will listen.

I know that there is more than enough for everyone. I know this because I am not as selfish as it has been stated some of those others were. I am smart enough to know that your dreams aren't going to be the same as mine. There's nothing wrong with that. Why should we have the same dreams? We are different people. Your idea of success may be nothing like mine. That's fine. I am teaching you how to improve your life in whatever way you want. I'm not going to teach you how to be me. That would be foolish.

Now then, if thoughts are particles that go out there, what happens to those thoughts? Do thoughts make things happen? Do thoughts join with other thoughts, come back to us and then we decide if we are going to take action or not. Think about this. Have you ever had an idea for an invention and sometime later you see it in the store? Have you noticed that songs you hear on the radio may have the same themes? I think it was the late seventies or early eighties, a lot of songs came out in quick succession about eyes? I mean they were different bands but there it was.

How many times have you thought of calling someone and they phoned you? I remember more than once picking up the phone to call someone and they were there. I mean the phone didn't even ring. I literally picked it up to call and that very person was already there.

How about that morning you woke and nothing went right? You stubbed your toe and that was it. You said this day will suck! Yes my friend that day did suck.

Remember the odd day when you just knew everything was going to be perfect that day? I mean nothing went wrong at all. The coffee was very good, the car didn't complain at all and started perfectly, at work everyone was nice, clients were wonderful? Just on and on.

Are you seeing the trend here? It's your thoughts that made all these things happen. There is no such thing as coincidence. Don't doubt me. How teachable am I? Key #2? Who do you listen to? Key #1. Stay with me!

I really want you to hang onto this idea. Your thoughts go out and make connections to other thoughts and put things into action. This is the beginning of you being able to live the life you want. The thoughts you put out make things happen. So what thoughts are you going to focus on? I suggest that you want to think about all the things you want to happen and push aside the negative thoughts. Start practicing. I will share with you the knowledge in detail as this program unfolds. For now just make an effort to place your thoughts on good things.

Don't fight the negative thoughts. Allow the positive thoughts. Think of it like this. When you are in a dark room, you don't fight the dark. You turn on the light and the dark goes away. Your thoughts work the same way. When you focus on the positive, the negative just goes away.

I have been asked if you have to believe in LOA. The answer is no. It always works. It has to always work. It's a law. Here is an example.

I worked in a large office. There was this lady who complained all the time. She would bitch about something that happened last night. Now sometimes these things were more serious and some weren't. I mean every day she had something bad to say. I was listening to her with a smile on my face. When she finished her story for that day I asked her if she ever had a good thing to say. She simply said, "No!"

We all laughed including her. As I really began to understand this information, I started watching those around me. It was very interesting.

This is one I think happens more for ladies. They attract the same kind of men over and over. They don't want that type of man but yet they get them. I'm sure this happens to men as well but in my experience it appears to be more prevalent in women.

I will show you how to avoid these traps. You are going to learn to attract all the good things. No it isn't hard but there are some things that you need to learn and do or apply in your day to day life.

So we accept that LOA is the most powerful law. This, my friend, explains how some people have 'everything' and others don't. The former attracted the good things.

Now comes a very hard hitting fact that you must understand. I can't decide where to introduce this into the program. It is perhaps the hardest thing for you to accept. Yet, once you do accept this you are well on your way to changing everything in your life. You will understand more and more as you go through this program. Here it is. You and only you attracted all the good and bad things that have happened in your life. You are completely responsible for everything that has happened so far. The great news is that you can change it. I mean you can change it all from now on.

Now I'm not going to say that you attracted serious bad things that may have happened when you were young. What I am saying is you have the power to attract good or bad and you have done so. It is automatic. It is the law. So you need to learn how to control it so that you can achieve your dreams.

People like to blame government, their childhood, lack of education, that they were picked on, bad parenting and on and on.

When you truly accept that you created everything in your life, then you will at that second become extremely powerful. You have no choice. If you can say, "I attracted everything in my life up until now and I can change anything I want." When you come to this level of understanding then you should be excited. Accept it without blame or judgment. Just accept it for what it is. Now learn how to change it all for the better.

Let me introduce a concept. If thoughts are particles as is proven. That's not just something I say; it is proven. Then think about this. Thoughts are energy. So, the energy you put out by your thoughts can be changed just as simply as changing the station on your radio. You just change your thoughts.

In LOA you may have heard about energy, frequency and vibration. You can use these words interchangeably if you want. The real statement is energy vibrates at a certain frequency. This energy goes through all known matter as it is smaller than the smallest thing out there. It is very powerful and does travel around the globe.

A great quote is, "You get what you think about most of the time" Earl Nightingale

Another, "Whatever the mind of man can conceive, and bring itself to believe, it can achieve." Napoleon Hill

Learn these quotes and hold them close to your heart. Re-read them right now! Don't move on until you have given them some serious consideration.

The first one, "You get what you think about most of the time" helps to explain that you don't have to worry about every single thought that goes through your head. However, you will get what you think about most of the time. If you think something bad or negative and you keep thinking about it, then it will come to you in some form. If you think of something bad or negative and you catch yourself doing so and you change your thoughts to something positive, that makes you feel good, or something you want then that is exactly what you are putting in motion. In short, think about what you want most of the time.

The second one breaks down like this, "Whatever the mind of man can conceive" means whatever you can think, "and bring itself to believe," you must believe it is possible, "it can achieve," you can have.

Do you doubt this to be true? How Teachable Am I? Are you willing to accept new thoughts and ideas? Are you teachable right now?

Earlier I did say that you don't need to believe in LOA right? Let me clear this point up right now. It is true; you don't need to believe in LOA. It is a law. But you can use it to change everything in your life and that, my friend, does require belief. "Whatever the mind of man can conceive, and bring itself to (believe), it can achieve." In order to attract something, you do have to believe that you can have that something. More about this later.

I don't believe that anything needs to be complex or difficult. So I say this in summary. LOA is just this simple; whatever thoughts and feelings you put out, you will get back. Like attracts like; birds of a feather do flock together.

So, let's now move on and learn more about the technique you will use to attract things.

Dream, believe and achieve whatever you want.

CHAPTER 7

Feeling Good

What is your main goal in life? The big one? The most important? I believe that everyone wants to feel good. Everyone wants to be happy and joyful all the time. Wouldn't you love the idea of a life where you wake in the morning and are excited to see what wondrous things that day holds for you? Seriously what do you want?

If you previously wrote down all the things you want, you may have written things like: Be wealthy, be a great parent, have a loving mate, be the greatest teacher, have a new car, increase my income, be healthy, have a great body and so on. All the things we want are designed to make us feel good. Really think about that. Everything you want is to make you feel good. How about that vacation you want to take some day. How many ways will that make you feel good?

Let me tell you something you need to know and take action on. You must feel good now! Yes, right now. You must feel good now with the goal of always feeling better. This is huge! This is vital.

There are 3 basic feelings. Feeling bad, feeling ok and feeling good. Yes, there are many degrees of feeling badly and feeling good. We are going to keep things simple so we will just agree that there are these 3 basic feelings.

If you feel badly to any degree then that is the frequency you are sending out. If you are feeling ok, then you are sending that feeling out there. When you are feeling great, that is the frequency you are sending.

Now if you feel bad and you are sending that frequency out, situations are going to happen to keep you feeling bad. If you are feeling ok or just average then you will have an ok life. This is what happened to me most of the time. I had an ok life but not exciting and amazing. I lived a lot of my life with no passion. I wasn't happy I was just ok.

So, if you are feeling great most of the time this is what will come back to you. Great things. We hardly ever think that what we do today comes back to us sooner or later. People have said many sayings more of an expression then meaningful. Watch what you think about you might just get it. Treat others as you want to be treated yourself. I'm sure you can come up with many more that you've heard as well. The point is, we hear this mouth noise but never really give it any thought. Well I am asking you from now on to give this some thought.

Think about this from now on. When you do or say something see if it doesn't come back to you. Every action you take will come back to you in some way. If you help someone, the next day or soon something you like will happen to you. If you are mean to someone then something will happen to you equally as bad. Just observe and be aware from now on.

You absolutely must feel good most of the time. If you want a wonderful life and have all the things that you want, then you must feel good. I do mean literally most of the time. Over 50% of the time Is this clear? Not just flickers of feeling good now and then. It isn't as hard as you might think.

Of course you can't control every thought that comes in to your head but you can decide just how long you will hold that thought. When you feel that you are getting angry or feeling bad in any way, Change that thought. Flip it to a positive loving or happy thought. You may have to practice this for the first while. Key four, the 4 Steps to learning. Soon you will be doing this automatically.

Most people think that they will feel better when they get what they want. This is a big reason why people don't get what they want. This is simply placing that old cart before the horse. It is totally backwards thinking.

In the last chapter you learned about your thoughts going out there and coming back to give you what you want. So, if you go around waiting to feel good then you will never feel good. The trick is to feel good now with the goal of feeling better. It is something you need to focus on every minute of every day. Yes, it really is that important.

If you simply walk around feeling good all day long, things will happen to keep you feeling good. Remember that lady who never had a good thing to say? She always felt bad so she attracted things that kept her feeling that way.

How about that happy go lucky person you know? They obviously feel good all the time so things happen in their lives to keep them feeling good.

This is so powerful! I love this concept. Just feel good. I will give you ideas later for how to do this so don't worry. Just get this in your head. Feel good all the time, as good as you can with the goal of always feeling better.

Now some have said to me, how can I feel good when I have this debt or that bad thing in my life. Yes, I understand this. I lived this. I went from kneeling before the tub washing clothes to living an amazing life. I was so unhappy in many ways. My relationship wasn't what I wanted. I didn't even have a job. The collection folks were calling for money and I didn't have any to give them. I was down and out. If someone told me then, Michael you have to feel good, I would have laughed at them. When I look back, I can quite clearly see the things I did do. I had no clue about any of this stuff at that time. I was just figuring things out bit by very little bit.

I remember putting the harness on my guide dog and going for a walk. I didn't have a destination, just went for a walk. The sun was shining and there was a light breeze. I stuck to quieter streets when possible. I listened to the birds. I could smell the grass. My dog was enjoying the walk too. She could feel I was picking up my pace and was ready to go faster. She picked it up too. My stiff and sore muscles in my back were loosening from washing the clothes in the tub. I started enjoying the day. I loved it. I stopped and hugged my dog. She leaned in to me, her way of hugging me back. I don't know how long we walked but I do know this, we got back to that little two room apartment and we felt a lot better.

I went from feeling broke and depressed up to a degree of feeling better. I won't say I was walking on air. The point is that I was feeling better. I don't expect that someone can go from being at the bottom of depression to absolute joy at once, however you can make steps. This is why your goal is to feel as good as you can now with the goal of always feeling better. You can do this. Really it isn't all that hard. Just make some progress every day. Let me be very clear on this. Make progress every minute of every day.

Giving is something that we can all do that makes us feel good. There are two types of giving and we must not confuse them. There is the giving that we feel we must do. Perhaps a collection plate or a particular charity at work. This is not the kind of giving I am talking about. I am talking about giving with joy. Giving without expectations. Giving from the heart.

I want to be very clear. I am not saying don't put money in the collection plate or donate at work. I am just using those as examples of feeling like you have to give and if there are any negative feelings associated with the giving then the chances are that the process may not work.

When you give with joy because you want to, it will make you feel good. It feels good to give. It doesn't have to be money. You can give of your time. Perhaps at a food bank, a place that provides food for less fortunate people. There are all kinds of volunteer work you can do. Of course you can give money as well. They say that when you give money from the heart you will get it back tenfold. What a nice thought that is. It makes total sense to me. When you give with joy, the universe has no choice but to give back to you in some way.

You can give a few moments of your time by helping someone who you don't even know. Hold the door open for strangers. Offer assistance if you see someone struggling with something. Not everyone will accept your offer of help but that's ok, many will.

Here is something just as important. The opposite of giving. This is receiving. I was very bad at receiving. I liked to give but I didn't like getting. It made me feel uncomfortable. Even something as small as buying me a cup of tea. Maybe I had this feeling of someone thinking I wasn't able to afford the 2 dollars for a cup of tea. Maybe I felt like I would then owe someone and I would have to balance that out later. I can't say for sure why but I didn't accept well at all. Not even birthday and Christmas gifts.

Here is the big news. You must be able to receive. It is vital to your success. If you put out a thought that you want something and you are not willing to open yourself up to receive it, you simply can't get it.

Remember Key #3? Where do I focus my thoughts? You don't ever think about how something will happen. You only think about the dream. If you want a new car and you aren't willing to open yourself up to receiving that new car in whatever manner the universe decides is the best way for you, there is only one option. You have to buy the car. Just let the car come to you.

I was teaching this idea to a student recently. There are two sides. Someone is giving and someone is receiving. I think we can all agree that giving is a very wonderful thing. So if someone is trying to give you something and you refuse that something, then that person wasn't able to give. That person may walk away feeling badly. Now if someone wants to buy me a cup of tea or whatever, I thank them and mean it. I offer up gratitude and that, my friend, is a very big win-win for both the giver and the receiver.

Something that is very important. If you think you need to wait until you get in order to give, you are thinking backwards. You see you must give in order to get. If you can give money, even a small amount, then you will get it back tenfold. You have to give while trusting in the process. You must listen to your heart and not the mind that is calculating down to the penny if you have enough. Now I am not saying you should give so much that you can't pay your bills as that would cause great stress. I am saying give what you can for now and as you get more give more. Many state that 10% is the magical number. I'm not so sure there is a magical number. I suppose giving 10% of your earnings is a good amount. The bottom line is that you have to feel good about it.

You can give in so many ways. Just be sure to do it with a feeling of love and joy and not feeling bad to any degree or even that feeling of just being ok.

You also want to pay attention to connecting the dots. When you are thinking bad thoughts and something bad happens to you then connect those dots. When you think and or give with love and joy then something good will happen to you, connect those dots. If you are involved in a negative bitch session and later on you get a parking ticket, connect those dots. The negative talk made you feel something, maybe anger, and the parking ticket gave you more of the same feeling.

If you are happy to help your kid do some homework and that was fun and you felt good then the next day someone buys you an unexpected coffee, connect those dots.

So often we go through life needing proof. The proof is there, it is always there. You just need to connect or link the two things together and you will see just how wonderfully simple it really is.

Yes, it feels good to give. It also feels very good to receive. So apply this in your life and watch and see what happens.

Here is a list of things that will make you feel better. This is in no way meant to be a complete list. They are simply ideas. You can implement the ones that work in your life. I fully expect that you will add to the list. These will be things that you already know make you feel good.

Think positive loving thoughts. Say how much you love things.

Move your Body

Go for a walk in the sun. While walking, look at things far away. I don't know why this works but it is a remarkable way to combat depression. It doesn't matter about the weather, just go. When you walk, hold your head up and walk briskly. Swing your arms.

Exercise. I have taught people how to lift weights and I will produce a fitness program for my clients. It is just that important. When you exercise you will feel better.

Dance. Just put on your music and dance. Again this is movement. If you are shy about dancing then do it when no one is around.

Listen to music. I am listening to music right now as I write this. I have a lot of music that simply makes me feel good. I have to say that Kenny Chesney has so many songs that make me feel great. He can put me on a beach and loving it. He can make me feel loved. He triggers so many emotions. I probably have most of his music. I sort them in themes. So when I want to feel more love, I play the loving songs. When I need to feel the sand, sea and sun, I play those songs. I had an MP3 player made for blind people. I loaded it up with music. I could walk down the halls at work and be a million miles away. Someday I will meet Kenny and thank him. So whatever music you enjoy, play it.

Be Creative

When you create something with your hands you tend to feel better.

Play a musical instrument or learn to. I play guitar and sing. When I really need a pick me up, I stand up and move as I play. You want to believe that the crowd enjoys it too. I just wish they would stop tearing off my shirt. Grin.

Make something with your hands. If you enjoy woodwork, build something. Get out the knitting needles and make something.

Play dough and plasticine is not just for kids you know. I can't pass one of those containers without making a silly little snake or a bowl.

Take painting lessons or draw something. Don't worry if it doesn't look just perfect. Enjoy it.

Cook something. If you enjoy cooking; some people get a great deal of joy from making food. Try a new recipe.

Pocket Full of Happies

This is one of the things I do very often. I have what I call a pocket full of happies. These are simply memories that I have. Might be a time in my life or holding a baby. I have several pictures in my mind that always make me feel good. I remember my old buddy Rod's reaction to his first rollercoaster ride. We are both blind. He asked his brother to put us on a smaller one and work our way up to the bigger ones. His brother put us on a big one right off, one which you didn't sit down on, no it was the standing up one. Well, all the way up when we realized which ride we were on, he was saying what he was going to do to his brother as soon as he got his hands on him. I had tears coming out of my eyes from laughing so hard the whole way up. I guess the ride was fun too but that wasn't the memorable part for me.

In your mind, have a list of pictures that no matter what makes you smile. You know these days we snap pictures of everything we do. So go back in the mental books of photos you have and remember those old pictures that make you feel good.

Remember old stories. I can vividly recall stories that my Uncle Ken told me. He's been gone now for years. I can hear his voice like it was yesterday; the laugh in his voice as he told a story.

I am sure you have many things you can place in your mental photo books. They will be sitting there just waiting for you to pull out when you need them.

Play Time

If you have kids, take the time to play with them. Talk silly with them. My Mom and I used to do this. I loved the mornings with her. I was an adult and we still did it. She would be making me some breakfast and I would lean against the counter and we would simply talk about silly things. One that jumps to mind is Mom and I were talking about how daring we were. She said she took a bite of an apple without washing it first. Man I said, "you live on the edge, well I jumped off the bottom step." We'd go on and on laughing. A very good start to any day.

If you have a pet, play with it. If you don't have a pet and it fits into your lifestyle, consider getting one. Talk to your pet. Pat them, brush them, hug them. Let them know you love them just as much as they love you. My last guide dog loved to be brushed. When I was done I had to tell him how handsome he looked and give him hugs. He would be wagging away and you could feel how much happier he was and it made me feel better too. When I began a grooming session it was a chore. But as that session went on we both enjoyed it.

Arm yourself and those around you with some sort of gun that shoots balls that are soft and can't hurt anyone. Get goggles to protect your eyes and just chase each other around. Try that after a dinner party sometime and watch the place liven up.

There's nothing wrong with being silly and acting immature. You will probably have more mental pictures and stories for your happy pocket too.

Emotions

Hug. Just hug. A handshake is nice but a hug is wonderful. I'll hug anyone. I don't care if they are men or women. To hug a friend gives you an amazing feeling. I know it's not socially acceptable these days but that's a sad commentary as far as I'm concerned. Hug your kids, pets, and your mate. Hug your friends if you think you can.

Want to change how you feel right now? I do this when I talk to schools or groups. I just get everyone to smile the biggest goofiest smile; the great big one. I mean from ear to ear. Look in a mirror and smile at yourself if you want. It is just that simple. Just smile. Go through your day and smile as often as you think of it. Smile at everyone you pass. Smiles are free but so meaningful. Don't worry about what others think, just smile at them. I bet often you will get a smile back. How wonderful is that? You feel better because you are smiling. At the same time you just made someone else smile and they feel better too.

Be enthusiastic. Stop with the hum drum behaviour. It doesn't matter what the task is that you are going to do. I mean the task has to be completed anyway. So be enthusiastic about it. Sing while you wash dishes. Dance with the laundry basket.

Raise your head, put those shoulders back. Stand proud. Just by changing the way you sit and stand, will change how you feel.

So I have given you quite a few things here. Some you can implement right now. You can come up with more things that fit in your life. I will now share things that you don't want to do. These will be things that make you feel bad. Obviously, that would go against what we are after in our goal of feeling as good as we can and to feel better all the time.

Things You Must Avoid

Opposite of saying loving things is speaking and thinking words of hate or anger. When you hear yourself saying you don't like something quickly change it to what you do like. I hate my job. I really do love some of my co-workers.

Do not listen to the news. Do not read the news. How many times have you felt good after listening to news. I haven't listened to news in years. I have missed nothing from doing so. Think about that. When is the last time you watched a newscast and felt good? It is filled so often with the most heinous of crimes. I was listening to someone crying after reading a terrible act from one human to another. I just don't get it. People have told me if you don't listen to the news then you are uninformed. Ok, I am uninformed about what? I create my own life. This is what I am teaching you to do. What can anyone possibly say on the news that I would find useful. You will understand this more and more as we go through the process. Just try this for a week or four. Avoid anything to do with the news. Yes, even on the car radio. Turn it down when the news comes on or pop on your music. See if you all of a sudden become ignorant. Of course you won't.

Do not get involved with negative talk. Negativity does breed negativity. As soon as I can, I change the topic.

Avoid negative people. No matter what, some people just insist on being negative. They will kill everything you are trying to do. I stopped some time ago participating in the 'Bitch Sessions'. I can't tell you how often I thanked that old MP3 player of mine. When I went for a break, I had the tunes up loud and was a long way away.

Avoid negative thoughts. When you find that you are thinking something negative, you will know by how you feel. If you feel bad, then you are thinking negative thoughts.

I use my body to tell me how I am feeling. If I bang my arm, I stop for a split second and say to myself, what was I just thinking? Most of the time it was a negative thought. I really like this one. It works well for me. Others have told me this works for them as well.

I would like you, for the next day or two, to pay attention to your thoughts and how they impact your feelings. Write them down in your journal. Watch for the markers that the universe is giving you to remind you to change your thoughts. Like me bumping my arm or banging my leg or something like that. Generally, it will give you the same feeling that you are thinking. When I bang my arm, it usually annoys me more than it hurts. So I was thinking about something to make me angry and banging my arm gave me more of that same feeling, anger.

Importance of Language

Some say that the words we use can work for us and against us. Well it's sort of true. I believe this to be true. The words are not the important thing. It's the attachment we have to that word that gives us the feeling.

I knew a guy who would complain and bitch all the time. I knew he wasn't being negative. Funny but he loved to bitch. He bitched about anything and everything. He did it with a smile on his face. If I did the same thing, I would have all kinds of negative things happen to me. His complaining was fun to him. To me it would be detrimental.

On the other hand, I knew a guy who would seriously complain. His previous wife was so and so, years after they were apart. One time we were out fishing in my boat. He was going on and on. I finally said stop! Look at where you are. You have the most beautiful day; we are where we love to be on a day like this in the boat. We have fish in the live well. The birds are singing. This, my friend, right here just can't be finer. He did stop. He took in a breath and started to laugh. The rest of that day and evening was perfect. We caught more fish and saw nature at her best. Perhaps I should clarify, he started catching fish finally. Did you get that? He wasn't catching fish until he changed his thoughts. I was catching fish though.

Just start by changing all negative thoughts or words to loving, enthusiastic, beautiful thoughts or words, whatever that means to you. Try to connect the dots of good thoughts with good results and bad things with bad results. This will be all the proof you will ever need.

The bottom line here is to feel good now. Feel good all the time with the goal of feeling better.

Dream, believe and be whatever you want.

CHAPTER 8

Gratitude

The subject of gratitude has been discussed in books and other forums. I can't help but wonder how many people are actually applying this so simple and rewarding technique?

You now know how important it is to feel good right now and to keep feeling better. Well gratitude helps this process but, more importantly, it will help you to attract things into your life at a much quicker rate. You must think about this often throughout your day.

You must put out this feeling of gratitude. You can do so in your mind. People around you need not know what you are doing. Yell it out in your mind. Really put out the thoughts with power. Smile hugely when you do so.

Whenever I ask for something and when I receive something, I offer up a thank you. Many times I say and feel thank you. This is easy I suppose but think of this for a moment. If the frequency we put out is what we get back then what do you suppose will happen when we put out the frequency of thank you, thank you, thank you throughout the day? Yes, you are right, situations, things and people will come into our lives to make us feel even more grateful.

The universe is nothing more complicated than a boomerang. A boomerang is an Australian Aboriginal weapon. When in the hands of someone who knows how to use it, it gets thrown much like a Frisbee.

The big difference is that the boomerang comes back. An old joke … What do you call a boomerang that doesn't come back? The answer is 'A stick'. So, the thoughts you send out come back to you. If you put out a powerful constant feeling of gratitude, the things, people and situations will come into your life to make you feel grateful.

Let's flip the coin for a moment. What if we don't offer gratitude? I believe that when we don't send out gratitude then we are often putting out a feeling of non-gratitude. This isn't good. This will affect how we think and feel. So, correct this by saying thank you all day long. Feel the gratitude. I mean really get that feeling of being grateful. This is such a simple process.

No matter who you are right now, no matter what situation you are in, you always have things around you to be grateful for. Don't shut down on me. How teachable are you? Key #2. Are you willing to change the way you think? I hope that by now you are seeing why these 4 Keys really are keys? If you don't know them off the top of your head right now, make sure you learn them. They are just so vital.

The question now is, what can you do to offer up gratitude more often? Here are some things you can do every day, it takes no time and will help you in ways you can't even imagine.

When you first wake up in the morning, well, maybe right after you smash your poor alarm clock, do this. Just lay there for a moment and say in your mind thank you. You can be grateful for things in your life no matter what your current situation is. Thank you for this pillow. Thank you for this sheet. Thank you for the blanket that kept me warm. Yes, even, thank you for this alarm clock for waking me up.

Happy Feet

I love this one. When you get out of bed and as you walk to the bathroom do the following. When one foot hits the floor say 'thank' and when your other foot hits the floor say 'you'. By doing this simple thing, you will say thank you many times as you walk.

Then as you go through your morning routine thank everything around you. Thank you for this tooth brush. Thank you for the hot water. Thank you for this shower. Thank you for the soap. Thank you for the shampoo.

Do you see how simple this is? You don't have to look for things to be grateful for, they are right there before you already. As you do this process, you should be feeling good, giving off a powerful feeling of gratitude. What a wonderful way to start your day.

Gratitude Walk

As I said previously, in the list of things that can make you feel good, to take a walk. Let's take that one step further. Yes, that was a joke! As you walk, look around you and find all kinds of things to be grateful for. I am so thankful that I can hear the birds singing. I am so grateful for that tree. I am so thankful for those flowers someone took the time to plant. Thank you for the light breeze. Thank you for the sight of those leaves moving gently.

Also as you walk, swing your arms. Move your body. Maybe move your head to the sound of the music you are listening to or singing in your head. Remember to also look at things far away. You just can't help but feel better and so grateful for all the things we take for granted.

In high school, I had a teacher who rode a motorcycle. He was quite religious. I never forgot a story he told us. He was riding to work on the highway and looked up to see a flock of birds in a perfect 'V' formation. Their wings were in exact synchronicity. He pulled off the highway and thanked God for that vision. It obviously touched him in a deep way because he felt he needed to offer up gratitude. I also remember some of my fellow students saying that this teacher was a little crazy. I wasn't so sure. Maybe he was on to something. As it turns out, he sure was.

As you go through your day, there are many times that you can be grateful. When you go to a store and buy something, don't just flip a little thank you to the person at the cash register. Really say thank you. It will very likely improve their day too. Perfect!

I like people's help in stores. I like to ask questions and learn about what I am buying. When I'm in an electronics store, I find the person who knows about the item I am looking to purchase. I always start by asking their name. I think this is important. Since I enjoy having fun all the time, I build relationships and crack jokes while we are talking. Not only can they tell me about the product but also answer other questions such as do you get many of these returned? The sales person has always answered this for me. When we are done, if not beforehand, I thank them for their time and I will often shake their hand too. I make sure they feel good when I leave. I may only thank that person once or twice but in my mind I am thanking them over and over as I walk to the counter to make my purchase.

Bed Time

Yes as you lay your head down for a few hours of sleep, remember to take a few minutes to be grateful for the things that happened that day. No matter what kind of day you had, there is always something to be grateful for. Expressing gratitude is something that will start your day off right and will help ease your mind to sleep. May you have the sweetest most relaxing sleep and dreams filled with love.

Be sure to include this simple and very enjoyable activity in your daily life. You will enjoy the benefits. It is just so simple and helps make you feel good too.

In thanking people during the day you also make them feel good. Thank your loved ones and always remember that they really are the most important people in your life.

I know this. I am so very grateful that you are trusting in me to teach you what you need to know to be successful. I am so very grateful for this opportunity. I appreciate you, I honor you and I am very thankful for you. Thank you.

Dream, believe and be whatever you want.

CHAPTER 9

Power of Belief

There are many things in life that you do not need to believe. The law of gravity being one. You toss something up and it will come down. You do not need to believe in the law of lift either. Just look up and see the birds flying and airplanes moving across the sky.

You don't even need to believe in the law of attraction. It just works all the time. I explained a bit about LOA in another chapter but if that's just out of your belief right now, that's more or less okay. I say more or less because it also tells me that you are not willing to accept change in the way you think about certain things - Key #2. However, let's just go with the thought that you don't believe in LOA. Again I say you don't have to. However, to change your life you do, most definitely have to believe in some things. This information is so important and necessary to your success that I dedicated a section of the book to this subject.

Let's start by remembering that famous quote. "Whatever the mind of man can conceive, and (bring itself to believe), it can achieve." Note again the brackets.

This quote simply means that whatever you can dream up, and believe, you will get. If you think this is too hard to believe, open up your mind. Just let it be that there are things you don't know right now.

How did I go from being single and living somewhere I didn't want to live, in a job that wrecked my hands and wasn't satisfying in many ways, being very depressed, didn't care if I lived or not, frail and very underweight as I didn't even care if I ate. How did I go from that to this life I have now? It happened in a matter of months, not years? I had to change my belief.

I didn't do this by sitting around and coming up with strategy after strategy. I didn't work really hard. I didn't even know where I was going to live and I sure didn't know who I would fall in love with. I didn't even know that I would be eating such amazing foods and enjoying a life of wealth. There were times in my life that I didn't even know I could have these things. Maybe you have felt that way. Maybe you still have some of those feelings now. Please trust me. You can change it all.

I want to remind you that I know you are very special. I know this because you got this program. You obviously want something more than what you have right now. You don't need to be the smartest person in class. You don't need to be educated or anything else. You do need to be teachable and you do need to have the belief that you control all the things good and bad in your life right now.

I explained that previously. About needing to understand that you are responsible for all the good and bad things in your life. You need to have that level of understanding and belief so that you can appreciate that you can and will change it all. Don't be judgemental about it; just know you have the power to be successful in whatever that means to you.

I don't want you to judge yourself. There is no need for blame here at all. While teaching this concept to some people they may get hung up on this point. "It's my fault, that means I am to blame."

I say no. It's never about the blame. It's about the power. If you have attracted that so called bad thing to happen then you can attract a very good thing to happen and you have, many times in fact. So, no blame here okay? Just know that you are way more powerful than you think you are.

Now then, given that the quote, "Whatever the mind of man can conceive, and bring itself to believe, it can achieve" is correct, you have to believe. What do you have to believe? You have to believe that what you want to attract is very possible.

You must totally believe that what you want to make happen is within your reach. You see, if you want a new car but you don't believe you can have a new car, then you will not get that new car. It's really just that simple.

I want to stop here for a moment. Remember, I stated that I am giving you the best and most complete information I can? Some of the great books can lead you down the wrong trail here and there. This does not make them bad books. It just means after you learn what I teach, you can read the books with a more educated eye and discard the bad or incorrect information others have given. Some say this bad information was given on purpose to keep the bulk of the population from being very successful. I really hope that isn't true. However, whatever the reason I will tell you to be aware of this.

Some books state that you should make your dream big. Make them huge. I absolutely disagree with this point. Understand this, there is no such thing as large and small in the universe. Only your beliefs make it so. However, back to my point, if you make your dream so big that you have no belief that it will come true then it won't manifest. It can't come to reality, it just can't, and you must believe it can come true for it to do so.

Here is an exercise to help you figure out what I mean. You really must do this. You will want to do this exercise every few weeks or so. Put it on your calendar now while you are thinking of it.

Do not do this on the computer. Get a blue pen and white paper if possible.

You are going to write a list of things. One per line or at least make room between them. Write down around 10 things you want. It may be to eat at a fancy restaurant, have a new car, take a trip, meet your soul mate, get a free cup of coffee, have a million dollars, get a better job, just anything. Go ahead now and write them down.

Ok, now that you have this list, I am trusting that you actually did write out a list. If not, don't move on until you do. Skipping this little exercise will not help you in any way. Key #1 - Who do I listen to?

Now, go down the list and mark them from 0 to 10. 0 being that you currently have no belief that it will come true, 10 being that you have total belief that it can come to you. Hint, when you look at that thing, how does it make you feel? If you feel good then you have a high belief. Go ahead and number the items.

Ok, now you probably have some that are 0 and you have others that are an 8, 9 or 10. Here is the point. Do not focus on the 0 to 7. They are not in your belief right now. You can focus on the 8, 9 or 10 items.

Don't feel disheartened. I am not saying that you can't have the so called bigger things on your list. I am saying that you need to start somewhere. When you have achieved the 8, 9 or 10 items, you can then see how the process works and you can attract the so called bigger things too. It's all about raising your belief.

Now that you have a few things to work with, here is what you can do. Focus on one thing; if possible a 10 item. Close your eyes and see yourself with that thing. Feel it, smell it if there are smells, if you can hold it in your hand then do so and see your hand not just any hand. Don't just see a picture of this item in your mind; be with it like you are part of the video. Now go ahead and do this.

When you open your eyes, you really should be feeling good. If you feel bad to any degree then you have doubt that you will ever get this item. If this happens then you need to pick something else out and do the same process. Doubt is the opposite of belief and will block your efforts to receive what you want.

I will take you through the process for something most, if not all of us, can understand. Don't worry if this is too big for you right now. I am just doing this to illustrate the process.

If you wanted a new car, here is how the process would go. You would close your eyes and see the car as you are walking up to it in your driveway. See how gorgeous it looks. Man what a car. It's mine all mine. Now feel the handle in your hand as you open the door. Get in. Smell that clean new car smell. Feel the seat and how comfortable it is. Start that baby up. Hear that engine. Wow! Put it in gear. See your hands on the wheel. I mean your hands, your rings, your skin, it's your hands on the wheel, not just any hands. Feel the power as you step on the gas. Listen to that amazing stereo. Boy that stereo sounds good. You are alone. There's no sales person with you. It's your car. You are starting it in your driveway not at the car dealer. This is truly an amazing car and it feels wonderful to drive. Now send out a huge feeling of gratitude several times for having the car of your dreams.

When you are done holding that in your mind, you should be smiling hugely. You should be feeling really good. You should feel a hundred times better now than you did before you started this exercise. If so, then you will get the car.

Do you see the level of depth you want to reach in visualizing that car? You can do this no matter what you want. If you want to eat at some fancy restaurant, close your eyes and see yourself walking in the door. You wait for a moment and then you are seated. You review the menu and choose something. You can see the food coming to you and smell it as it is placed before you. You can see your hands picking up the utensils and eating it. You can taste it.

If you want a vacation, see all the things in your mind that you will see when you are there. Smell the local plants or sea, hear the exotic birds singing and so on.

Take it down to the deepest depth you can reach. Include all the details and play a part personally, don't just watch yourself from the sideline. See it as if you are doing it. At the end always give up as much gratitude as you can. Really send it out there with power.

So again I say, when you stop the process and you don't feel great, then you don't have enough belief that what you want can come true. Doubt feels bad, belief feels great. Always go with your feelings.

Expect

I teach that you act as if you have what you want right now. Perhaps the final step in the process of attracting something is to also expect it. This may be helpful to you. Again this is the opposite of doubt. If you put it out there that you have the new car but it follows with no expectation, then you probably doubt that you can have the new car. This is similar to being open to receiving something.

Something else that is very exciting. Once you put out the thought of what you want, you will begin to see it right away. Sometimes it will appear like magic immediately and other times it will come in bits and pieces. The point is you will see manifestations very quickly. Be aware of them, expect them and know that it is coming to you. Usually in ways you can't even imagine. Key #3, where do I focus my thoughts - never on the how, always on the dream or thoughts!

There are many ways to increase your belief that you can have something. Practice of course being the best way. If you believe that you can get a good parking space at the store then ask for it and see what you get. You can practice this all day long. More about this later.

Often we don't believe that we can have something because we have been told we can't. Maybe somewhere along the way someone we know said that you aren't smart enough to have blah blah?

One that comes up often in my work with others is rich people are bad people. They are mean and selfish, you don't ever want to be rich. Only show-offs drive that kind of car. That big home is a waste of space. A personal chef? You can't have one of those. A fit and healthy body? How will you do that? Your body runs in the family. On and on it goes.

Some well-meaning people really planted some nasty seeds in our lives. These nasty seeds have grown to become limiting beliefs.

Limiting beliefs are beliefs that stop us from dreaming, believing and achieving what we want. They are the voice in our heads that say you can't do this, you can't have that. What makes you think you're so good.

Think about this. I am blind and can't hear well either. I was never expected to amount to much. Well, I think I did believe that nonsense for a while. Ok, for decades actually. Now I have people who pay me big money to hear what I have to tell them. People who barely know me love me for the work I do. People know that I am passionate about helping them reach their goals. I make a difference in people's lives. I am a rock star every time I step out in front of a group of people at a seminar. I certainly wasn't supposed to do all that. Heck, I was lucky just to get a decent enough job. None of this could have come true until I got rid of my limiting beliefs.

There are a number of techniques for eliminating limiting beliefs. The one I use is called Emotional Freedom Technique (EFT) or tapping. It is a necessary tool to remove doubts and of course limiting beliefs. It is used in many ways but I am just keeping to this topic for now. I do plan to have some materials for my clients. I suggest you get on my email list so I can share more about the various supporting programs I have available to help you. There will also be announcements of seminars I will hold or attend and other goodies. This link will be at the end of the book. There are other techniques out there but I can't say that they are more powerful or better than tapping.

Remember the chapter on fears? Sometimes we can just simply take action or change the way we think and the limiting beliefs will melt away. This is not always the case. Some things are just too hard to get rid of without a system to blow away those negative thoughts and limiting beliefs.

So make sure you know that you will very likely need something to help you crush that negative voice in your head, the fear in your guts, and the doubt that you can have something. Be willing to live Key #2, always.

I hope you can clearly see why you must believe in the process for it to work. It is really quite a simple process. I am laying the foundation for you to learn and most importantly apply what you have learned. Yes, I want you to read this book over and over. Read it a hundred times and then again. Every time you read it, you will learn something new. Please don't be just a student. Take the information I have given you and take action. In taking action and practicing over and over, you will get better and better and more powerful. You can and will make a difference in your life. I want, no I beg you to do this. My reward is in your success. I love hearing how applying this information has made amazing differences in your life.

Some people have asked me about this information challenging their current beliefs. Some are not sure that this information may go against their religious beliefs. I don't think that it will. In fact I have been told that religious texts state things like: Ask and you shall receive, ask not and receive not.

I tend to believe that applying this information is very much agreeing with the basics of religion. Now understand that I am not an expert in that field. I will not argue one way or the other. I just don't understand how wanting to be happy and successful in whatever that means to you can be a bad thing. Also remember that not everyone has the same dreams. Not everyone wants the same things. Some just want to be the most amazing parent in the world. Well, this program teaches you how to be just that. Some want a successful business. No problem. Everyone I think wants to be happy and feel good and to help their fellow man.

The little knowledge I have about religion seems to agree with that. Ultimately, this will be for you to decide of course.

So in this chapter we learned about the vital importance of the power of belief. We must believe in order to achieve.

Dream, believe and be whatever you want.

CHAPTER 10

3 Methods to Attract

There are three methods to attract what you want:

1. Be very specific
2. Be general
3. Just feel good

All three of these methods work. However, understanding which method to apply for certain things will greatly assist you in getting what you want. I'm not sure that other programs describe these methods. In fact, I have read some books that say you must know exactly what you want, be very specific when it should come in and what you are going to give up to make this happen.

Ok, that does sound good. Know what you want. Sure. Know when it will come in. Yeah. What are you going to exchange for this to happen. Hmm ... First I will explain the three methods and then I will revisit this. I am sure you guessed by now that I don't believe that this is quite the right method to attract something. Now let's look at the 3 methods that do work.

1. Be very specific.
    To be very specific, you will want something with such detail that there is no doubt precisely what it is that you want. Perhaps you want

a certain ring. Only that ring will do. That is the ring that lights you up. There really isn't anything wrong with wanting that ring. But it is important that you are not super specific with a lot of things.

When you are so specific on some items, you are not allowing the universe to do its job. You may believe that this particular ring is the one for you. Let me ask you this, have you seen and tried on every ring in the world? Of course not! Just know that when you are attracting something specific, you are limiting yourself to other options.

Is it bad to attract something with a high degree of specificity? The answer is no. It just means that you will get what you want, exactly what you want. Nothing more and nothing less.

There may very well be some things that you want and if so then this is the best method. However, there are some things that you most definitely don't want to be so specific about. Suppose you are very attracted to a certain person. You start working on that person using this technique. You can attract that person. However, the best way to attract a lot of things is in the next section. I think you will understand after you have read it.

2. Be general.

This is often the best way to attract something. When you are being general, you are allowing the universe to decide what is best for you. If you want a new car, you can just put it out there that you want a new car with some specific features. That ring, you may want a ring that makes you feel good every time you look at it. People will notice that ring. When attracting your love, you may think that person is the one you want. Believe me, you are simply not that smart. Let the universe deliver the person who is best for you.

It works this way. When you want something and you are very excited about that something, you are obsessed about having that something but you are not specific, meaning a certain brand/make/model, a ring, or a love of your life, then the something that you want, wants you. You see if you want a specific car but maybe that car won't suit you for reasons you can't know, the universe will give you the car that is best for you. If you want that ring, the universe may provide one that's even better, one you've never seen before. A love of your life that wants you makes the strongest, long lasting fulfilling relationship you can imagine. Often being general is the better way to get what you really want.

Let's see if I can clear this up a little more. One of the things I want is a Rolls Royce. I've read about them. I've heard about them. They are sort of a symbol of wealth to me. Mostly though, I like a smooth ride as I don't like being in cars much so I feel that if I surround myself in luxury and all the safety features I can get and have my own driver, then I will feel better about being in a car. Here is what I have done recently.

I started thinking about the car that I want. I decided that I want a very high end car that is so comfortable to sit in with lots of leg room and an amazing sound system. I then considered, is it really a Rolls I want? Well the answer is no. I want a luxury car. How do I know what is the best make for me? I have no idea. What car is the best for me? So after I was finished slapping myself some, I changed my dream. I want an amazing car that is very comfortable, safe, lots of room, easy to handle for the driver, has all the bells and whistles I would enjoy, feels so nice to touch with wood and soft textures and so on. Do I know if that will be a Rolls? I have no clue, not a clue at all. I haven't even been in one. I haven't been in a lot of other luxury cars either. So I changed my dream. By-the-way, this is not a dream that I am super obsessed about right now. My primary dream is getting this amazing book into the hands of millions of people who will take action and make a difference in their lives. So the fancy car will come but that's really on the back burner for now. I've just given this as an example for how I was being too specific, especially when I don't even have enough knowledge about luxury cars. Just as you don't have any idea about that person who you 'think' will be the right one for you.

So, yes, I most definitely think that being general is the way to attract most things.

Here is how you would meet your love. I would hold that someone special in my mind until I could feel her there with me in the same room. I can feel that I could reach out and hook my long ape arm around her and pull her into me. I hold that feeling for a long time. I do this as often as I can every day for as long as I can hold the thoughts and feelings. I never once will think how I will meet her. I never put any limits on her. I write down most if not every day about the things I want in my soul mate but I never once focus on how I would find her.

Here is a story for you romantic types. About 18 years ago I met a lady who hired me for my first good job. This was after trying for those two years I spoke of earlier in this book. When she called me to set up an interview I knew we had some sort of connection. I had no doubt I would get the job. I did get the job and it was the break I needed to prove myself in the sighted world.

Over the next weeks and months Janice and I became very close. I was falling in love with her. I had a wife and a baby then so I didn't take any action. I think we held hands once. We had a lot of good conversation as we would often ride to work together. We could read each other's thoughts. It was almost scary. We were very good friends. I guess I thought maybe she felt the same way but we never talked about it.

Well eventually I moved up to the next job in a different organization. Then I moved across the country and we just lost touch with each other. I would think about her from time to time and wonder what life would be like to be with her. My wife and I weren't soul mates but we had a pretty good marriage.

Very recently, 18 years later, I found myself single again and I was ok with it. I had been thinking about Janice again. How I would love to be that close to someone. I have been thinking about her traits. The ones I loved so much. Intelligent, funny, quick witted, the softness of a woman but not needy. I went over my list of things that I wanted in a love again to see if I was missing anything.

Did you catch that? I was very specific on what I wanted in the love of my life. I was just not specific at all on who it would be or how I would meet her. I was really thinking about her traits. Key #3, Where Do I focus my thoughts.

Less than one week later on Valentine's Day Janice sent me an email just saying hello and to see what I've been up to. I told her that I was single and asked if she was too. She was. Within a couple of days we were loving each other just like we were back then. Only now we can explore what we have. The universe brought us together. As it always does, in the perfect timing for both of us. We will be seeing each other in a few days. Now, will I say that we are going to be together for the rest of our lives? No, of course not. Am I going to follow what the universe has put in front of us. You bet I will. If things between us flows naturally and easily then it is definitely worth pursuing. If we only see blocks and barriers, then the match probably wouldn't work. Frankly I have no doubt that we will have an amazing life together.

To give you an idea of how to be specific about things here is what I did. I wrote down all the things I wanted in the love of my life. They included being very intelligent, someone who could stand beside me, is healthy and health conscious, understands the law of attraction, enjoys the same music as I do, is very affectionate, we enjoy many of the same activities, we have amazing sex and so on. You can see how I focused on things that I wanted and not on things I don't want. I never said I don't want someone who is bitchy. It is important to always focus on what you want and never on what you don't want. What you really want, you get that. What you really don't want, you'll get that too. So my list went on and discussed all the romantic things, the loving things and the fun things.

As you can see, I was very specific in what I wanted but left the universe to bring it all together. So again, you must decide just what you need to be very specific on and what you can be general about.

3. Just feel good.

This is for people who really don't know what they want but they do know that they want a happy wonderful life. You can have that. If you go around and just feel good all the time, what will happen? Things, people, and situations will come into your life to make you feel good. The better you feel then the better things will be. This is a wonderful way to live. It's what we all want anyway. Isn't that why we want the cars, fancy homes, or more money and so on? It's designed to make you feel great! So go around feeling great. You know already that you must feel good now with the goal of always feeling better, right? You better know that by now. If you don't, then go back and learn that lesson.

You can't attract anything wonderful into your life unless you feel good now and keep feeling better. Do this every second of every single day. You can't have the money unless you put out the thoughts and feelings of having money. The past is gone and you don't know what the future holds. There is only now. It's true, there's only right now, that is why it's called 'the present'.

I always find it interesting how people's lives change when they make that one simple improvement. They just start feeling good. It makes a difference like you wouldn't believe. You know my story … blind, can't hear that well, had a mostly unsatisfying existence, didn't have a real reason to get out of bed. Now I feel good. I smile most of the time. I enjoy many simple things in my life like hearing the waves roll in, listening to birds, singing and listening to music and playing my guitar sometimes. I teach people, I write books, I make audios and videos, I have a great passion to help others, and I love life and the people in it. I got this from focusing on feeling good and working on feeling better.

Yes, I did have some dreams. That is what I wanted. It is foolish for me to assume that you want the same things. Maybe you have different dreams, nothing wrong with that. If you just want a great life, you can simply achieve it by feeling great all the time and having the only goal of feeling better. How can you not have a wonderful life? The universe will ensure that wonderful things happen to you. How amazing is that?

I do want to caution you about something. Earlier in this book, I said to watch those happy go lucky type of people; those who are happy all the time. I bet they are also successful. Well, not everyone who appears happy is really all that happy.

I knew a lady who was always cracking jokes and laughing. That was really nothing more than an act. At home she was alone and miserable. She was someone who I learned this lesson from. I am sure that it is very common. I think there are a lot of people like this.

You can't ever know what is really going on inside someone else's head and heart. You can't possibly know if a person is happy all the time or just putting up a good front. You do know how you feel though. You absolutely can change how you feel.

I think that if someone is happy all the time and has a wonderful life then they are probably a good example to model yourself after.

Remember, I said I would revisit this? Know what you want. Sure. You must know what you want. However, do you need to be very specific or general?

Know when it will come in. No way. This is part of the how side of Key #3. Besides due dates or timelines can stop you dead in your tracks. Timelines often give us stress. You don't know when the best time for something to happen is. Maybe the love of your life is moving into your area in a month from now and is not even on your radar yet.

What are you going to exchange for this to happen. Who's to say that you have to exchange anything? Who says you have to pay anything? Who says you have to sacrifice or give something up? That's just crazy. And yet I have read this. Sure you may have to give something up but this is off your radar so no sense in trying to focus on it let alone work out what it is that you have to give up. There's simply no good reason to focus on this and you might not have to give anything up at all!

Man I really do love all this information. Again I say I am so grateful that you are reading this book and will continue to the end and then start right back at the beginning and keep reading it over and over. I am so proud of you. Thank you so much. Apply what you are learning so you can make significant differences in your life as well as those around you.

Now then, I have explained to you the three methods to attract something. It is very important to know the difference and when to apply which method for what it is you are attracting. I trust that you can see how knowing the correct method will speed up your success and give you what you really want.

One further thing … If you are very specific about something and you attracted it and then realized that you don't really want it, not to worry. You just attract something different. Yes, it is just that easy. Switch the thoughts and feelings you are sending out and things will change. It is really such a fun game. That's what life should be anyway, fun!!!

Dream, believe and achieve whatever you want.

CHAPTER 11

Visualization & Intention

This is fun. It can be quite a lot of fun really. These are things you can do to help you attract what you want. I suggest you try them all and find the ones that work best for you.

The ones that work best for you are the ones that make you feel good. If for some reason it doesn't feel good then you are pretty certain that one is not right for you at this time. Like with anything else, this may change over time so you will want to test them all every now and then.

Now you've probably heard these suggestions before. Did you take action on them? Even if you did then I really want you to do so again. If you've never tried these techniques before then go ahead and give them a shot. Remember, it's not only important to learn this information, it is most important to put the knowledge into practice.

Vision Board

This is a board that you place on a wall where you will see it often. You draw or find pictures in magazines or online of things you want. You paste these things onto the board. It works like this. When you see the board you should feel really good and it should make you smile. For some people this is vital. It will also remind you to think about what you want, to think about the dream you want to happen.

The board does not need to be anything expensive. Just something you can hang on a wall and tape or glue pictures or drawings onto. Think about where you will locate the board. Someplace you will see it as often as possible. You sure can have more than one board if you want; one in your bedroom, one on the back of the washroom door, and one above the TV in the living room. Just anywhere you want. I think another great place is in front of any exercise equipment you may have. Maybe it will keep you there a little longer as well. Talk about a win-win!

You can have the picture on your computer and other devices as screen savers or backgrounds. Place them in your car. Have one on your desk. Be creative with this. I think you will find this a fun process.

If you are looking online, I believe you can just right click on a picture and either save it to your computer or maybe you can print it at that time. Just ask any kid and they can probably tell you how to get pictures off the internet.

Visualization or Meditation

This is when you sit back, relax and see it in your mind. We did do this previously. You are with the thing you want. Not just seeing a still picture of it. You are actually there and using it, tasting it, walking through that home, driving the car, spending all that money, feeling the sun and smelling the salt water on that vacation, holding your soul mate, feeling the feelings of having that strong healthy lean body. Really be in the moment.

When you are done and come back to the room, you should feel a lot better than you did before you began. You will also feel more relaxed as well. If you feel badly for some reason, this is because you have doubt that you can have it. If you do feel badly then you must figure out why. Is it because of something someone said, is it just out of your belief right now? Either tap that feeling away or change your dream to something you do believe in so you can have it right now.

Some tell me that they are just not good at visualizing things in their head. That's fine. Just sit back, close your eyes and pretend you can. It may take a bit of practice but I know you can do this.

Of all the tips I give here I think this may be the most helpful in attracting what you want. I also plan to record some meditations designed to help you in this process.

Just to give you an idea of how powerful this can be. I read a study about three groups of people tossing basketballs in a basket. They all took turns and the number of baskets made was recorded.

Group 1 were told to come to the gym and practice.

Group 2 were told to go home and practice shooting hoops but only in their minds.

Group 3 were told to go home and live their lives as they normally would.

After a set time they all returned.

Group 1 who actually practiced improved. No surprise there.

Group 2 who only practiced in their minds improved almost as much as group 1.

Group 3 made no improvement at all.

I found this stunning. Group 2 did nothing but practice in their minds and yet they improved almost as much as those who went to the gym and practiced. So this leads me to sit back and think about that. I came to the same realization that has since been proven. The mind can't tell the difference between what's real and what's not.

So if this is true which it is, this is why you can dream, believe and achieve anything you want. When you are living in the dream of what you want, your mind has no idea that it isn't currently true. Remember this? There is only the present? Ok, this is why it works so well. You live in the dream sending out the frequency of what you want and the universe has no choice but to make it happen.

A study was done where they hooked people up to a machine that measured muscle reaction. They asked those people to think they are running. The muscles in their bodies reacted very much the same as if they were actually running. Again, this proves that the mind doesn't know the difference from what is real to what is not. I think this is incredible. Since the mind can't tell the difference then you are free to live the life you want or have the things you want in your mind. This is why you feel so good when you meditate or think about what you want or more correctly, thinking in the present that you already have it.

Try this for fun. In your mind, go to the fridge and get a lemon. Hold it in your hand, feel it there. Feel how cold it is. Now take a bite. Did that just pucker up your face? Did your mouth start to water?

I was in my thirties and was ice skating with a friend of mine. Denis learned how to skate as an adult. Yes, he went out there with all the little kids and learned from a teacher. I always respected him for that. I was a good skater in that I could skate forwards and stop on a dime. I didn't know how to do other things on skates though. He would show me something and sometimes I would get it but not always. The next Sunday we would be back out on the ice and I had it down. He said a funny thing then that I never forgot. "I know you aren't practicing on ice. Are you practicing in your sleep"? The answer is that he was close. Maybe in my sleep too, I don't know. But I did practice in my mind. This was years before I ever began my studies in LOA. Interesting!

If you haven't heard of this type of story before, I suggest you do some research online. There are documented studies of someone getting rid of tumors. They have the ultra sound picture of it and then it is gone. The person visualized being healthy, they felt good about that and the tumor simply went away. Some stories talk about how a person was told he only had a short time to live. He decided to go out in laughter. He did nothing but watch funny shows, movies and comedians, and his disease went away. Yes, laughter really is the best medicine.

I could probably write a book just on the topic of visualization. I don't really think that writing such a book is necessary though. I strongly suggest you try this and give yourself some time if you feel you aren't very good at it the first time. Just relax and breathe deeply and slowly, clear your mind of all other thoughts and see what happens. I concentrate on my breath when I do this. It helps me to get the garbage out of my head. Once I am relaxed, I then bring the dreams into my mind and body. Play with this process and have fun.

Gratitude Rock

You now know the importance of offering up gratitude. I love this one. Don't be surprised if you see these on my website as well. A gratitude rock is simply a rock that you carry around in your pocket. When you reach in that pocket and touch it you are reminded then and there to think of things to be grateful for. When I hold mine, I swear I can feel warmth from it.

Think about this. Many Indigenous cultures had various dances to attract something. Be it a rain dance, sun dance and yes even war dances. I bet that more often than not the dances did get results. Why? That's easy; their minds were focused on what they wanted for an extended amount of time. That sure sounds like LOA to me. Even though I teach LOA from a more factual, or some say a more scientific, approach I do find myself enjoying the more spiritual side of things too.

I was talking with a Native Indian one time about LOA and I mentioned that in their culture they used it sort of unknowingly; the various dances and things. She agreed. I said, I bet when they wanted rain, they were able to attract it before the white man came along. You see before white man came along and impacted their core beliefs, these wonderfully spiritual folks had total belief. It was an interesting conversation.

Whenever I touch my rock, I hold it in my hand and in my mind say things like: I am so grateful for the sunshine, thank you for the birds singing, thank you for my family and so on. It is a very powerful reminder to smile and feel good.

Cheque from the Universe

This is a fun thing to do for those who want to attract money. Get a piece of paper and cut it to the size of a cheque. Put all the information that a cheque would normally have on it. It is a cheque made out to you from the universe. The amount needs to be an amount that feels good to you. This means you have to have a 10 belief that you can have that amount of money. Now fold it up and stick it in your pocket. Like the gratitude rock when you reach in that pocket smile and believe that you have that amount of money and will get around to cashing it. Remember to say thank you for this cheque every time you touch it. Be sure to have it somewhere where you will see and touch it often during the day.

Internet Viewing

Look at things online. If you want a nice home, then look at nice homes online. If you want to be wealthy then research all the wealthy type things. Look at cars, boats, yachts, and anything that means wealth to you. Don't look at the prices as that just doesn't matter. This can be very fun and make a huge difference for you. The reason this works is that it raises your belief that you can have these things. If someone else can then why can't you. Of course you can. Now like with anything else if this practice makes you feel bad then don't do it.

Touch What You Want

Yes it is good to look at pictures and vital to visualize. If possible, go and be with the thing you want. If it is something tangible like a car then go car shopping. Touch it, feel it, get in it and be with it.

If you want a nicer home then take a drive around town and look at the kind of homes you want. If one is for sale then get a tour of the house. Again be with it. Get your belief way up there.

If possible, get a picture of yourself with the thing you want. Even a video, why not! Talk about raising your belief.

Here is something that is very important so I want to be very clear about it. You must be obsessed and feel good. To be obsessed means that you think about it all the time. To feel good means that you must send out the feeling of what you want with great passion and excitement. This is so necessary. If you just put out the thought of wanting something but not really being very excited about it then you won't get it. Always remember to do this in the present tense.

Take the time to try these methods and be your amazing successful self. Play the game and be obsessed.

Dream, believe and be whatever you want.

CHAPTER 12

The Simple Procedure

This is a fairly short chapter. It is summing up what you have learned. If you skipped the rest of the book to come here, you won't understand the process. There's a lot to learn. The previous chapters teach you what you must know to reach high levels of success. You can't just short cut your way through this and get results.

If I were to step out the process it would look like this:

1. Feel good all the time.
2. Be grateful now.
3. Give and be open to receiving.
4. Have a chief goal, that one thing you want the most.
5. Should this goal be specific or general?
6. Believe you can have it, absolute belief.
7. Be obsessed, think about that dream as many times every day as you can for at least 2 to 3 minutes each time.
8. Take action when opportunities come up. Be very aware of nudges from the universe.
9. Be grateful, put out a feeling of gratitude for having what you want.

You see, it really is just this simple. It is the human mind that gets in our way. We complicate things. I am certain you have been writing out the 4 Keys and know them by heart now. The whole thing revolves around those keys. They will keep you focused and on track.

Here is how the human mind complicates things. We listen to bad information from the wrong people. Key #1 right?

We are not teachable and therefore won't allow ourselves to just keep things simple and change the way we think and act. We don't take the time to master new information. Well that's Key #2.

We focus on the how and not the dream. I can't do that! How can I have this or that! Where do I focus my thoughts, sounds like Key #3 to me.

What do I know right now? Am I proficient in this process? Am I practicing what I have learned? Am I allowing myself to change? Can I do this without thinking yet? Do I still need to think the process through? Do I even know yet? Well that's Key #4, the four steps to learning in reverse.

You can see that this whole thing is just so simple. Don't complicate it. Get rid of the negative emotions and thoughts by thinking good and positive thoughts. Use a releasing technique every day for anything that comes up. I suggest that you should tap (EFT) every night before bed. What a great way to end the day.

I will go over the above steps and expand on them as a reminder for you.

1. Feel good all the time.

I have stated this several times. Feel as good as you can now with the goal of feeling better. Reach into that mental pocket full of happies. Enjoy everything you do. Be enthusiastic, stand proud and walk with purpose. Work on motion and emotion.

2. Be grateful now.

Always offer up gratitude. Say thank you in your mind. Scream it out with great feeling and power. Take gratitude walks. Do the happy feet. There are so many things to be grateful for, it's all around you.

3. Give and be open to receiving.

Be sure that you are giving. Your time, money and so on and be very open to receiving. Be sure you are able to receive graciously. Again this was an issue for me. I was not good at receiving. It was something I had to consciously work on. I never had a problem with giving though.

4.   Have a chief goal, that one thing you want the most.

I think this is a failing point for a lot of people. They scatter their thoughts over so many different things so nothing much ever happens for them. You really must have a main goal. That one thing you are going to really focus on. What is that one thing you want most. Once you have that, need it, desire it, be with it, and be obsessed over it.

5.   Should this goal be specific or general?

Decide if it would be better for the universe to choose what is right for you. In most cases, this is the best way. It is also very fun. Say I don't know how this is going to work out but it will be interesting to see.

6.   Believe you can have it, absolute belief.

If you have any doubt, your thoughts will push the desire away. So, dream, believe, achieve.

7.   Be obsessed, think about that dream as many times every day as you can for at least 2 to 3 minutes each time.

Do everything you can to think about that dream. Vision boards, meditate, and so on. Again, remember to think about it in the present. You must feel as though you have it right now.

8.   Take action when opportunities comes up. Be very aware of nudges from the universe.

Be aware when the universe is trying to tell you something. Some call this intuition, raising your antenna, gut feelings, nudges, even ideas. The point is, be aware and when you get an offer to do something and it feels right and good then do it. There are times when you must take action. Don't force something. It must flow and go smoothly.

9.   Be grateful, put out a feeling of gratitude for having what you want.

You can't put out too much gratitude. Before you rejoin the so called real world, while you still have the feeling of what you want, really pump out that feeling of being grateful for having it.

I hope this overview was helpful. Can you see just how silly simple the whole process really is? This should be taught in schools. How the world would be so much better if we knew this information as children.

Be amazing and dream, believe and achieve what you want.

CHAPTER 13

Playing with this Information

As you know, there are no big things or small things in the universe. This means that you can attract anything you want. It all comes back to your beliefs. If you believe something is too big, perhaps an amount of money, then you won't get it.

Yes, I know, some books and people will tell you to make your dream big and even make them huge! The problem with this is what if you have some big dream, what if you think you are doing everything correctly, what if you don't see the dream manifest? Well it's play time.

You can play with this technique all day long. I encourage you to do just that. In playing with things that aren't so big and important to you right now will be vital to your success later.

I was in an airport. I wanted to catch an earlier flight. It didn't really matter to my life if I got the earlier flight. I just wanted to get home a couple of hours sooner and didn't really want to sit in an airport for more time than I had to.

I asked if there was an earlier flight. The gent informed me that there was but it was full. I thanked him, smiled and went back to my seat. I thought about how good it felt to be home sooner. I just felt good and enjoyed my thoughts. About 15 minutes later the gent asked me what colour my bag was? I have no idea what happened. I didn't focus on how I would get on that earlier plane. I was very grateful and got the result I wanted.

Another trip I was taking. The flight left late. So I landed late and I needed to catch a connecting flight or it would make things very difficult. I had to go through customs and other security stuff and my guide, an airport employee was saying there's no way we are going to make my flight. I felt my braille watch and told him not a problem. He was arguing with me. I told him to just watch and see. It was so amazing how quickly I got cleared and we arrived just in time for me to board the plane. The guide was saying how he's never gone through customs so fast and he couldn't believe that we made it in time. I laughed. You know how it happened, I felt good. I knew I was going to be on that flight and I was so grateful for being on my flight.

So you can play too. There are lots of times when you can play. Below is a short list to give you some ideas.

Parking space. Now this is fun. When you are on your way to the store, put out the dream or thoughts of having a great parking space when you get there. Does it really matter all that much if you get one? Probably not. It will be nice though. So ask the universe for a great parking space and feel good when you do so and for goodness sake, don't yell at other drivers on the way. Just sing with the music and feel good all the way there. If you did get the great parking space, remember how you attracted it. Think about how you felt the whole way to the store. Conversely, if you didn't get a great parking space then review how you felt on the way to the store. Were you thinking negative thoughts? Were you arguing with someone? Did you even believe that you really could get a good parking space?

Remember the defeatist thoughts? "I knew I wouldn't get a good parking space." You must change the way you think. There's Key #2 again.

My dad does this. Mom was telling me that she never gets a good parking spot but your dad does. I know he expects a good parking spot when he gets to the bank or where ever he is going. I've been with him many times and witnessed it for myself.

How about this, I want a free coffee. Again it doesn't matter if you get one or not so there is simply no stress. Maybe you will get one that day, maybe the next day, who knows. I've done this once in a while. Often it would happen the same day. Sometimes it was the next day and when it happened I remember thinking, perfect! I really would enjoy one right now. Mine was a tea though. Sorry, I'm not a coffee guy. Grin. I never ever gave it a thought as to how I would get a free tea or anything, it just happened. Key #3.

Go ahead and attract ten dollars. It's only ten dollars. It will be fun to see how it comes to you. Picture a ten dollar bill in your hand and know that it will come. If your belief isn't strong enough for ten dollars, then 5 dollars or one dollar. It's just a game.

This may be a little more stressful for you but again it's worth playing with. In your mind, dictate the outcome to conversations. This could be any conversation at all. If you are going to a store to return something and you don't know if they will take it back. Don't be in a confrontational mood when you walk up. You have already put out there what you want the outcome to be. If you see the meeting as going bad, have your arguments all lined up and that you are going to get angry, then that is very likely what will happen. Instead focus on the outcome you want, be patient, ask questions and smile, and then see what happens. At the very least, it should be a win win!

I think a reminder here is useful. There are no good or bad experiences. It's really very true. There are expected and unexpected outcomes though. When something unexpected or so called bad happens to me I don't get upset. Not anymore. I simply say, "Ok, this doesn't feel very good. Maybe this happened because the universe has something better in store for me. I don't know how but I know it's all going to work out for me."

I will ask myself, how am I feeling? Have I been thinking negative thoughts and attracting this experience to myself? If the answer is no, then it is just part of the plan that I don't know yet. It's ok. Because I know that I can change it. I have the power to live by design, my design. So do you!

The person who wants a better job may get fired or somehow lose their job. Often one can't get a better job while they are working at the job they dislike. So yes, it does seem bad that this person lost their job but I encourage that person to say I don't know how but I know this is going to work out for me. This person must believe it and feel good about it.

Perhaps you are going to a restaurant. Just know that you are going to get great service and have a wonderful meal. Know this ahead of time and watch and see what happens.

I have been to this one restaurant a few times. There was always something wrong. They didn't bring the right food, it was cold, just something. It got to the point where I expected something to be wrong. I felt it before I got there and even while I placed my order. Yes, it never did work out right. I don't live in that town now or I would go back and put everything into practice just to see what the outcome would be. I have no doubt though that I would get great service and good food. My thinking would make it so.

This is why it is so important to focus on feeling good all the time. It is just as important to have a means of stopping those bad feelings when they come up. A releasing technique like tapping or a pocket full of happies that can instantly change how you feel. This could be things like a picture in your head that you just can't help but smile at no matter what, as previously discussed.

Remember, to dream, believe and achieve anything you want means that you are living life by design and not some sort of random way you have probably been living it so far. Know what you want. Feel good about it and watch it happen. Just go ahead and play. Have fun. That's what life is all about, having fun.

Dream, believe and achieve whatever you want.

CHAPTER 14

More Things to Do

This chapter will have more things that you will want to consider implementing to help increase the intensity of the energy you send out. These are simple ideas that we should all follow as much as possible for our health as well as our mental wellbeing.

Exercise

I know this was mentioned previously but I want to give you some ideas for things you can do.

Joining a gym or having one at home is going to be the best of course. However, if that's not your thing then I will give you some tips. Yes, I do plan to provide my clients with various programs later so be sure to join my email list.

If you join a gym, always use the free weights. I feel very strongly about this. I have used very expensive machines in very modern gyms. They are not as beneficial as using free weights. Just to explain, free weights are the hand held dumbbells and bars. When you lift with free weights you are training muscles that can't be trained using machines because the machines do a lot of the work for you. Safety is number one for me and I think it should be for you too. As long as you are lifting correctly and only the amount of weight you can lift properly then you will be perfectly safe. I have trained in public gyms, even on my own, and I've never been injured by lifting weights. It is a good idea to get a personal trainer to teach you the proper technique even if using machines. However, you do not need a personal trainer to set you up on programs and to follow you around. They can be very expensive to hire and not necessary at all. I will have some programs that I will suggest. Be sure to get on my email list. The link is at the beginning and end of this book.

Yes, ladies, you get in there and lift weights. If anything, it is more vital for women to lift weights. The stronger the muscle, the stronger the connected bone is. This means that if you lift weights you will definitely reduce the chance of Osteoporosis. This has been proven. I knew about this decades ago.

Before you say it ladies. You won't get big ugly muscles. Want to see me rant? Come to a seminar and ask me about you getting big muscles if you start to lift weights. I will go off. Grin. Here's the deal. If you start to lift weights and get big ugly muscles then stop lifting. The muscles will shrink back down. There is a very small population of women who will get bigger muscles but this is very much the exception.

If you choose not to join a gym then I plan to have an exercise program using your body weight and some light dumbbells. This is a very inexpensive option and you can follow me right from the comfort of your own home.

You can join fitness classes. I think a very good one for anyone to join is Tai Chi. This is a form of martial arts. It involves slow graceful movements that are designed to give you some flexibility and improves balance. No impact and you aren't breaking boards or anything like that. It is very relaxing.

There are lots of classes for a variety of age groups and your current fitness level. Who knows, you may even make some new fun friends.

If you want to buy some equipment here are some thoughts for you to consider. The first question I ask someone is, what do you like to do? If you like riding a bike then get an exercise bike. I am not a fan of running. I believe that people over 20 years old should never run. It is just too hard on the body. The pounding of your feet can hurt your feet, shins, knees, hips, back and even your neck. If you are a runner and don't have any problems, then continue to run but get regular physical check-ups to ensure you aren't wearing out your joints.

I like low to no impact machines. My personal favourite is the Concept 2 row machine. I like the model D. The only real difference with the upgraded model E is that it is higher off the floor. There are some other minor differences. I have never tried the model E. the advantage of it being higher means it is easier to get on and off the machine.

I also got the kit that allows me to connect my phone to the row machine. I can update my rowed pieces from the phone to the Concept 2 website.

I suggest you spend time on their site and learn more about the various products they have available.

This row machine works all the major muscle groups and will last forever. Relatively speaking they aren't very expensive. Not for the quality you get. Also Concept 2's service does not end at the purchase like most other companies. Check out their website, concept2.com. I can't say enough about these guys. Weightlifting is also called resistance training and you can increase the resistance on this rower and it still runs smoothly. Resistance will make you stronger which as you learned will make your bones stronger.

Other machines that are very safe are: elliptical or orbital machines. You stand on them and sort of walk but your feet never leave the peddles. No pounding at all. Some have handles to work your arms as well.

If considering an exercise bike be sure you do some checking on them. Some you sit and lean back and some you sit on like a standard bicycle. A tip for anyone who rides a bike, exercise or not, make sure the seat is wide enough for the bones of your bottom to sit on. If you get off your bike and anything down there is numb you can be doing some nerve damage.

I have used a stair stepping machine. The only downside is that they only work your legs. This is true of the bikes as well. Working your whole body is always best. Used correctly, these machines have no impact. They will give you a good cardio workout as well.

This is important to keep in mind. Before you buy something, go to the store several times and really workout on the machine you are considering purchasing. They shouldn't mind. This way you can get to know that machine and be sure you are getting the right one for you. Also gym equipment stores will almost never take anything back. So be sure to ask them about their return policy. If they do take it back, it won't be at full value. I do think that Concept 2 does have a 30 or 60 day in your house return policy. That is if you order directly from Concept 2 and not at a fitness store.

Walking

Going for walks is very good. Walk briskly enough so that you are breathing a bit heavier and swing your arms. Wear good shoes to reduce the pounding. I like running shoes with the heels higher than the toes. A lot of cushion as well. When walking look at things far away. This is a very relaxing thing to do and who knows what interesting sights you will see along the way. Enjoy Mother Nature, she has so much to show us. Try to walk for 30 to 60 minutes two or three times a week. Also send out the feeling of gratitude as you are walking.

Massage

Getting a massage once a week is very good for lots of reasons. Get a full body massage. Among other benefits, this helps to eliminate stress and to detox tissues. Who's kidding who? It just feels good.

Inversion Table

Consider an inversion table. I have one and like it. You lock your ankles in and lean back on the table. You can make it invert so you are hanging upside down. You don't need to flip all the way upside down if you don't want to. It helps in a lot of ways. Some say they have eliminated various back issues on these tables. I do feel better after using mine even if just for a few minutes.

Mini Trampoline or Rebounder

I have not tried one yet though I do plan to. These are little trampolines that you have in your home and you gently bounce on it. It is supposed to help drain limp nodes and have other benefits as well.

Medication

This is very serious. Many parts of the world are so drugged it is shocking. We get a sniffle, off to the drug store for some pills or nasal something or whatever. It's ok to have a cold. Frankly when you start implementing various things in this chapter you will probably not be as ill but if you are, it's okay. Do not use any over the counter stuff if you don't absolutely need to.

I am not suggesting that you stop prescription medications, I am not a doctor and I will not tell you what is good or bad. All I will say is to eliminate as many medications as you can. They weaken us. I know some older folks that are on so many medications, they are even on medications to offset other medications. That's just crazy to me. Work with your doctor and maybe even consider getting a second opinion. Do some research on your own. I could go on and on about this subject.

Food

This is a big hairy beast of a subject. I know, I had a fitness site once. I talked with many people about what to eat and what not to eat. I have read lots of books and reviewed many websites. Perhaps there is more information about this topic than any other. Things I taught people years ago are now coming up in the news as suggestions we should follow. I shake my head. Main stream news is just so far behind. Anyway, let me make it as simple for you as I can.

Eat anything you want that is as close to Mother Nature intended. This means if man turned it in to something else it probably isn't fit for human consumption.

Eat foods in their natural state. Fresh foods. Whole foods. If you eat meat, get the whole meat not deli meats and organically grown when possible.

Don't kid yourself into thinking that man-made cereal is good for you. Think about this. When man fortifies foods by adding back vitamins and things, do you really believe that the food is going to be good for you? I don't.

Flour is a huge no no. It doesn't matter if it is whole grain or not. Breads, cookies, buns, anything with flour. Healthy muffin? Not a chance.

The chemicals in processed food are scary as are the fertilisers in the ground or sprayed on our food. MSG must be avoided.

Eat organic whenever possible but at least eat fresh foods. Raw is best. Greens, you can eat lots and lots of those. The darker the green the better.

I encourage you to do some research of your own on the internet. There are countless clinical studies and other research studies about overuse of medications, the dangers of processed food and that which has been grown or raised on chemically fertilised ground.

I believe that dairy products are not good for human consumption. I think that this food should be avoided. I believe I once heard Brian Clement from Hippocrates Health Institute state that cow's milk will cause more lung cancer then smoking. This makes sense to me. It's the mucus or flem that causes a lot of illness and dairy causes flem. When I attended the school for the blind, I drank huge amounts of milk. I always had a cold. Mom took me to the doctor and said that I was sick all the time. They ran tests and took x-rays. They couldn't find anything of course.

I know when I eat cheese I get a lot of pimples. Just something to think about.

If you really want to be healthy and eat cheaply, I suggest you research these folks ... Hippocrates Health Institute at hippocratesinst. org. I do plan on spending a few weeks there. I know a lot but I still have much more to learn. They have helped people suffering from major illnesses for 50 or 60 years. Key #1. Who do I listen to? I will listen to these guys every single time. Of course there's no sense if you are not willing to change, Key #2. Their diet is very simple and very inexpensive and incredibly healthy. The sad thing is that most people will not eat this amazing diet. At least not until they are diagnosed with some horrible disease.

I was just saying to my lady love last night. Do you know what the biggest problem we have with illnesses and obesity and so on is? We humans have a twisted view about food. Here is the skinny on food. It is a fuel. It is nothing more and nothing less. Thanks to advertising and traditions, we humans have made food a bigger thing than it really is.

It's just fuel. Give that some thought. Perhaps you can start choosing the better fuel for your body.

Vitamins

I am not an expert in this area but here's what I think. Most of the time when we take vitamins, we aren't even absorbing them. Then there are those who take this vitamin and that supplement and so on. I know you need to be concerned with one supplement interacting negatively with others.

A good way to go is to look into taking whole food supplements. They say it is taking food and putting it in a concentrated form. If you are eating very clean foods, as nature intended, you probably don't need to take anything. However, if you feel you must take something then this is probably the better choice over chemically made vitamins. Nothing chemical is good for you!

Sauna

Have a sauna. The director from Hippocrates Health Institute has a sauna 365 days a year. I have heard many of their interviews. Check out YouTube for an interview with Dr Mercola and Brian Clement. Brian is the director and shares a lot of information with Dr Mercola. There are some advantages to an infra-red sauna.

Detox

This too is a controversial subject. How to best detox? I can't say I really know the answer. Brian Clement talks about this in his interview I mentioned above. If you are not willing to go whole hog and learn from Hippocrates Health Institute, there are different detox programs you can get. When you do some research in this area you will find various detoxes. Some for lungs, heavy metals and lots of other organs in the body. Again this is something you very well may want to consider.

Truth Testing

This is a very exciting technique that you can learn. I am familiar with it, though I won't call myself an expert so I won't teach it at this time. This is a method of muscle testing that once mastered you can use it for all kinds of things. You can test to see if a food is safe to eat, determine if someone is telling you the truth and even test for the suitability of pets before you get one. In fact you can even scan the animal when it is ill to figure out what the problem is. I do plan to really take some time to master this.

Did you know that there is something called a healing crisis? If you have something that is supposed to be good for you like a magnetic necklace or anything like that and you have it on all the time, you can actually be placing your body at risk. With Truth Testing you can determine if you need the necklace right now and for how long you should wear it. If doctors and pharmacists learned this, they could test people for suitability of medication and never overdose anyone again. You can learn more about this at www.quantumtechniques.com. Dr Stephen P. Daniels, the director of Quantum Techniques has taken tapping to another level. I have communicated directly with him and worked with one of his staff. I think these folks do amazing work.

The idea is to have the body as clean and strong as possible in order to increase your power. Some of these ideas you could probably implement right away. Others you may wish to research and do what feels right for you. Remember your keys and give these tips serious consideration.

Dream, believe and achieve whatever you want.

CHAPTER 15

Further Information and Answers

In this chapter I am going to address some situations that may come up. It is sort of a question and answer section where I hope to touch on any concerns you may have along the way.

Right off the top, here is one I often get asked. Michael, what if I'm doing everything right and things don't work out for me? Chances are this won't happen however, if it does give this some thought. First thing to consider, are you feeling good. If you are feeling good and I don't mean just acting like you are feeling good but you really do feel good, then if something doesn't work the way you think it should, sit back and give all of these factors consideration.

Do you really know the 4 Keys? Can you write them down off the top of your head? Are you applying them?

Do you even know what you want? If you have no direction and you expect an outcome then how can the universe get you there? You must have that one primary thing that you want. Focus on that thing as often as you can throughout the day with power, feeling good, for at least 2 to 3 minutes each time. Understand this; you must have one primary goal. I have seen too many times where people don't focus on that one thing and become obsessed about having it. They scatter their thoughts over too many things and do not give any one dream much power.

Are you doing all the things we talked about? Are you going for walks, getting some sunshine, eating well, using the vision boards, meditating, not taking over the counter medications including headache pills, enjoying your life, reading and re-reading this book. A little tip. I read my own book often. Yes, it is a good reminder for me even though I wrote it.

Are you avoiding listening and reading the news, staying away from negative people and not talking or thinking negatively about anyone? This includes things that people post on Facebook.

A lady I was teaching told me about a guy who often posts terrible things on his Facebook page. I could hear in her voice that it upset her. The answer was obvious. Unfriend him for now and continue building your life the way you want it to be. Key #2 right? Are you willing to change? What are you willing to give up to make a difference in your life?

Now let's just assume you are doing all the things correctly and you still aren't getting results. Here is the point. If you are being too specific and things just appear to be too much of a struggle, then it probably isn't the correct path for you to travel.

What if something bad happens?

I don't view things in the light of good and bad so much anymore. I think of it as different experiences. If I have a so called bad thing happen I know I attracted it. I review how I've been feeling and thinking. If I have been stewing on something bad then I attracted it. If not then I wonder, if this didn't go the way I expected then it must mean that the universe has something better in mind for me. Sometimes you simply have to burn everything down in order to rebuild again. Like the person who wants a better job. That person loses their job. Fine, now the door is open to get a better job or to start their own business and so on.

How about this ... You are driving along and you get some sort of break down. A flat or something like that. I would not say how bad this is. Again, if you aren't angry then the universe is doing this for a reason. Get excited about it. Maybe you will meet someone new and have a new friend. Maybe it is exactly what you needed. Maybe something up the road a bit was going to happen and by being delayed you are not going to get in an accident. Maybe the car stopping just saved your life. You don't know. Just feel grateful and say, "I don't know how or why but I know that this is going to work out best for me."

I will touch on relationships for a moment. I plan to write another book on attracting the love of your life. It is such a big topic.

I decided I would join one of those free online dating sites. I met the odd lady who was very nice. This one lady though, she was amazing. She was sweet and we really hit it off. I thought that she was a very good possibility. I was careful not to use my teachings to swing her my way. I kept focused on the things I wanted out of a relationship. It turned out that she wasn't interested in me, at least not enough. I then re-read all the things I wanted in my love. She fit a lot of the things I wrote about but not all of it. In fact, some of the most important things to me were missing. So you see I was blinded by her sweetness and how well we got along. I know she will make some other man very happy, just not me. Had I forced the issue using the techniques to attract her specifically, we would have had a mediocre warm relationship. Not one of passion that I have now.

So be careful. If you are single, then write out what you want in a love and you will know the right one by how well they fit everything you have written. Be sure to write everything in the present tense and always in the positive. Don't write, I don't want someone who is abusive. Remember, what you really want, you will get that, and what you really don't want, you will get that too. So focus on the wants.

A reminder about positive and negative energy. It is true that positive energy is much stronger than negative energy. However, consider this, if you put out what you don't want in a very strong manner filled with anger and the wrong side of passion then of course you will get that.

A note on present tense. You should always act as though you have it now. Whatever it is. If you think how nice it will be when you have … that is in the future. You can't ever catch up with the future and therefore, whatever you want will remain in the future. Think about that for a minute. If you say I'm going to … It will stay just ahead of you and you will never catch up with it.

I was explaining this to a friend recently. There were three things on the table. I lined them up with a bit of space between them. I said this is the past. I tossed it away. The past is in the past. We can't change it so we move on. Now I have two things remaining. One was the present and the other the future.

I had one in each hand. If you say, I'm going to have it looks like this. I then moved the two things across the table like one was chasing the other but never catching up. The present was chasing the future. then I tossed the future away. This left only the present in my hand. All we have is now. Nothing else matters but now. I have …

This is why it is vital to feel good now with the goal to keep feeling better. You believe you have it now. Just like those folks who practiced shooting baskets in their minds and improved. Just like taking a bite of that imaginary lemon and your face puckered up. Just like the folks who thought they were running and their minds and the machine registered their muscles sparking as if they were really running. The mind doesn't know the difference between what is real and what is not.

Never focus on the past. The past simply doesn't matter. A minute later that is the past. It doesn't matter where you came from and all the negative things that may have happened to you. Go ahead and change it all. You know how. You probably already are seeing manifestations.

I thought this was quite interesting. I was on a call with some of the friends from that group a while back. There were five or ten people and someone asked me if they should write their life story. I knew her history and it wasn't a nice story to tell. I replied absolutely not. Then the discussion began and others said that it could be therapeutic. Still others said that it would be good for people to know your story as perhaps they too could learn from it. I asked her why did you ask the question? She told me about someone who was teaching something similar to this information. He stated that in order to move on you must know where you came from. I disagree vehemently. The only thing it would do is make her relive all the bad things that happened in her life. If that's not thinking negatively then I don't know what is. You see we can and do change our thoughts in an instant. Therefore, the energy we put out changes in an instant. Thinking about what you want in a powerful positive way will bring you what you want. Reliving the past will only attract more of that bad stuff.

Yes, I know I told you in this book some of the struggles I've had in my life. I did so to help you see where I was and where I am now. Trust me, I didn't write hardly anything about my life. I didn't want to relive it and I think I told you enough of what you needed to know so that you can see the changes I've made in my life.

If it were her goal to write a book to help others go through the experiences she had and to come out a better person in the end, I would say write it down. However, her goal was to learn how to attract something. Key #1 should be screaming in your head right now.

How do you know when you are beginning to see things happening or as some say manifestations? Say you want a new car. You will start seeing that car all over the place. You may see it in ads, on the streets, in shows or movies, just everywhere.

More about what I call nudges. Some call this intuition or perhaps inner voice and I'm sure there are lots of other words for it. Gut feel is another one. Whatever you wish to call it, here's how it works. When you want something and you really desire it, you are burning to have it. You need to be aware of nudges from the universe.

Some stories I have heard about people getting an idea and acting on it. One lady had this crazy urge to turn down a street she has never been on before, then to turn again. She ended up pulling up in front of a place that hired her. Sure, some people would think that's crazy. I don't. Not at all! I think it's wonderful. She didn't think about the how. She just thought about getting the job and followed the nudges.

One of my clients sent me an email saying she overheard someone in an airport talking about playing a slot machine. Something inside told her that was a good idea. She didn't even know how to use one. The voice in her head told her to bet $20. Well she couldn't bring herself to quite spend that much so she put $5. Of course she won. She was not as excited about the winnings as she was that she followed her little voice and saw results. I can't tell you how proud I am of her that she learned this lesson.

A word about giving. Remember, there are two kinds of giving. One is when you are obligated to give something, usually money. The other is when you are moved to give because it feels right to you. It makes you feel good.

Obviously feeling obligated to give something isn't going to give you either the pleasure or the results as if you give with joy.

I have heard that whatever you give willingly and with joy you will get back tenfold. I believe this is true. I suggest we all give. Be it money, blood, time or anything else you feel moved to give. When you give from the heart, you feel good. You are doing something good. How can this not come back to you in a wonderful way.

I have given freely of my time many times. I like to do most of this sort of thing secretly. I don't need recognition in any way, it just makes me feel good. It's that simple.

Don't be surprised if you get an email inviting you to a free webinar that I hold. You see it gives me so much pleasure to teach this information. I really want and need you to make a difference in your life. I will send out some free videos as well. Who knows what else I will do. Just make sure you join my email list so I can keep in touch with you.

Do not take this whole process so very seriously. One of my clients was stuck. He was so concerned that he didn't know just how his life should end up. In the chapter about playing with this information I talked about this. It's about learning how to attract something. It is an enjoyable process. You don't have to map out just how your entire life should be. Start smaller and make things happen. Understand the process through having some early successes. This will raise your belief and will allow you to have a better idea of how you want your life to go. Besides, if you attract something and you don't like it then change your thoughts and attract something else. Never get stuck.

The main reason you need to read this book a hundred times is this. You are learning. So when you are learning you are at some starting point. As you go through this information the most important bit of knowledge you need right now is what will jump out at you. The next time you read the book, something else will be the most important thing you need. You see, every time you read this book you are changing. That's what knowledge does to us. It changes us. We grow a little more.

Think about this for a moment. Have you seen a movie or read a book you haven't read in years? Now when you watch that movie it seems like a different movie. Obviously, the book or movie hasn't changed. You are the one who changed. It is your life's experience that made you read that book with a new level of understanding or a different eye.

I love reading books. I have reread many books over the years. Some are novels I read for the pleasure of it. I can see that my understanding of the book is so much deeper now than it was back when I was much younger. Some books I like even more now. I read a book in high school for English class. I won't name the book, I just don't like being mean about someone else's work. I didn't like the book then. To be honest, I really didn't like that book. Well, in the last year or so, I decided I would give it another chance and read it again. No, I still really don't like it. Grin. So sometimes a book can get better and other times they remain in the list of those I won't read again.

I trust this helped to answer some of your questions. Again, I suggest you join my email list. I will have various means for you to get in touch with me. This may be a webinar, seminar or online chat. This way you will have an opportunity to ask me questions you may have.

Dream, believe and achieve whatever you want.

CHAPTER 16

More on Thoughts

I just read something that I thought was very interesting. It was quoted as being stated by Ken McFarland that 2% of people actually think, 3% of people think they think and 95% don't think at all.

What does this mean? Well probably all your life you haven't really been thinking. You have been reacting and working on what you have been told or learned. Sure, we have senses that gather information for us. Sight, sound, smell and touch. That's not thinking. If anything that is just perception.

I used to be one of the 95%. I have no doubt of this at all!

I was a reasonably smart person sure. I never thought that I could ever have the life I wanted. I just didn't think it could be possible. So I lived a small life. It wasn't a bad life but certainly not what I have now.

We have been taught so many bad things by those who never intended it to be harmful or limiting to us. They taught us to be grateful for what you have and don't expect anymore. Ever heard, you should be satisfied with what you have? I recall hearing that a number of times in my life.

I ask this. Why should I be satisfied with what I have now? Does this mean I can't grow? I can't achieve something else? I should have continued working in tremendous pain and be satisfied with that money?

No way! I will never be satisfied. I will be and always am very grateful but satisfied, never!

You see the amazing thing about being a human is that we can grow and become better and better. In fact, some say that when we stop growing we are dying. So never stay in one place. I am quite certain you know this by now. This whole book is about teaching you how to dream, believe and achieve whatever you want. Then are you done? Of course not! You can achieve new dreams. That's what makes this so exciting.

Right now I am writing this book. It will reach millions of people. They will learn how to live the life of their dreams. Am I done? Not a chance. I have so many things to do. I have so many dreams to fulfill. That to me is what makes life fun and exciting.

Think about all the things you know of that you probably take for granted. Huge buildings, incredible bridges, even athletic records that have been broken. Just anything you can see or think of. It all had to start with love for something and a dream.

These things were not achieved by people who didn't love or think. In other words, these things didn't happen by accident. It took a dream and passion. There was intent and yes, thoughts.

This book is here to teach you how to think; how to activate your thoughts so you can live your dreams. You can plan your life. Yes, you can live by design and no longer as a floating bubble or follower.

Again I want to say how proud of you I am. You have made it all the way to the end of this book. Well, almost to the end. You are not only one of the few people who did so; you are also one of the few who have been taught how to think. You have joined the 2% of thinking people. You know you have to read and re-read and read this book some more. It's so true. Don't stop now. Believe me, you have so much more to learn from these pages. I encourage you to keep this book with you always. Be amazing!

Let's take a few minutes to review how you ARE thinking differently than you were before getting this book.

In chapter 4, the four keys gave you a guide on how to think, things to be aware of and a new way of thinking about things.

In chapter 5, you learned not to live in fear but rather to live in love. The opposite of fear is love. You also learned to take action and not to have a defeatist attitude … probably, a new way for you to think.

In chapter 6, you learned a bit about LOA. Some call this the big secret. You learned that your thoughts are real things that go out there and mix with other thoughts and come back to give you what you think about most of the time.

In chapter 7, you learned the importance of feeling good. This again is teaching you how to think. Yes, the focus is on your feelings but what are feelings without thoughts? You have to think about feeling good before you can feel good in most cases.

Chapter 8 talks about gratitude. This too is a new way to think for most people. When you think about how grateful you are then more things will happen to keep you feeling grateful. A beautiful circle indeed!

In chapter 9, you learned about belief. You must believe to achieve anything. What is belief other than simply changing our thoughts to accept that we can have something.

In chapter 10 you learned about the 3 methods to attract something. How best to think about IT. Do you do so with specificity, in general or simply just feeling good all the time?

In chapter 11 we talked about the different methods you can apply to help keep your thoughts on what it is that you want. Vision boards and so on.

In chapter 12, I outlined the simple procedure; stepped out the process to show you how to think.

In chapter 13 we talked about how to play with this information. Reinforcing the thought processes.

So you see, by learning and applying all this information you can't help but become one of the 2% of thinkers. It's not possible that you won't. You are not only learning to think but how to think. You can think your way in to a life of design. How wonderful is that!

I say congratulations! You are wonderful.

Dream, believe and achieve whatever you want.

CHAPTER 17

Money

Perhaps I will write a book just on the subject of money. Frankly, you have all the tools in this book to attract as much money as you want. However, there are things you should know if you want to increase the amount of money you currently have.

First thing is, you have to love money. You need to desire money. You must be obsessed about money. Think about it in the present tense. It's the same process that we have gone over before.

As an employee in most jobs you are on a set amount of money. No matter how hard you work you will still get that amount of money. In some places you may be able to take on more responsibility and get more money. This would be a pay raise or promotion. That is just fact.

If you want real money, big money, then you will want to consider starting your own business. Obviously with the internet there are many options to make money in your spare time. You can do so with little money down. Not like before the internet when you would usually have to rent a store or location and go from there.

If you have a passion like I do then follow that passion. As you know for me it is teaching. I have a need, not just a want, but a desire to teach you how to make a difference in your life. How to dream, believe and achieve whatever you want. This burns in me. In fact it took me a very long time to write this book. I mentioned previously that my hands are injured. So I can't write all day. If I could, this book would have been completed in days not months. It just doesn't matter. I know that this book is getting done and it will help people. I think about this book all the time. I love this book. It is going to be my launching pad to everything else I do such as audios, videos, other programs and so on. All the things I can do to help you realize your dreams. This excites me. Therefore, it will happen and it can't help but be successful.

Many people have taken their hobbies and turned them into businesses. Everyone has knowledge about something. Write a book about that knowledge. People need to know what you know.

Think back, what did you always want to do? When you were a kid, what did you want to do? I am giving you absolute full permission to view things with a child's excitement. Like you did before everyone took that wonderful ability and crushed it. Dream those dreams, believe them and achieve them.

A word of warning. Be sure you know what you want. If one of those things is to have lots of free time then do something that doesn't require you to work 14 hour days. Mind you, if you are doing something that you love then a 14 hour day is not a problem at all.

You see, I won't open a store. I don't want to have to open and close the shop while being there all day long. I don't want to work that many hours. If this is your dream then go for it! Just follow your passion.

Think about this. You should never work for money. The only reason you should work is to feel good. Some people find this in their job. Example, someone goes to college and becomes a teacher. They love walking into their school and classroom. They love the challenge of reaching kid's minds and having them understand a new concept. That is their reward. It really doesn't have anything to do with the pay they get every two weeks. I've met teachers like this. It is so easy to see the difference between a teacher who is teaching because they love to and those who are just collecting their pay. It's passion. It's always about the passion.

If you want a certain amount of money each month then focus on that just like getting a car or anything else. You can do it this way. When you focus on the money, you will get ideas leading you to the money.

Act on things. We discussed that before. Be aware of the nudges and take action. If it feels good then do it.

I've been asked what if it doesn't feel good anymore. That is probably the time to get out and find something new. We are human. As humans we have the wonderful ability to grow. What your passion was last year doesn't have to be your passion this year? Just be sure that if it doesn't feel good anymore that you understand the reason why. If it feels like it is getting too hard then why is it going that way? Are your thoughts right? Are you focusing on feeling good or are you thinking negative thoughts? You need to check that all the time.

I used to fish. I mean every chance I got I would be out in the boat. It was about catching fish sure, it was really about being out there and enjoying the water and birds and stuff like that. I was learning more and more about fishing and I came across this guy who had an internet business about catching fish. Not just fish in general but a specific kind of fish. I bought his program and even chatted with him. You could clearly see his passion in everything that he did. He interviewed professional fishermen who were also passionate about catching fish. What makes a pro fishermen a pro? Easy, they win some tournaments and state they are an expert. You want to bet that these pros are using LOA knowingly or not to catch the big one.

There are people out there who make a ton of money in selling their knitting programs online. I used to be able to crochet but I was never a knit whit. I couldn't knit if my life depended on it. Grin.

As with all things, you want to have that same feeling about money as you do everything else. Be excited about it. Think about it all the time and expect it to come in. Don't get worried about when it will come in. It will come when you are ready to receive it.

Just like everything else you can be specific or general or just feel good about money. I really didn't focus on amounts. I simply walked around putting it out there that I am so incredibly wealthy. I could feel it. Later when I set up the online business I will have targets. Specific amounts. Will I worry about not reaching those amounts? Of course not. It will be a fun game.

I read a story about a gent who wrote a book. He decided that he would have a certain amount of sales that would net him $100,000. He reached over $95,000. He was just short of the goal he set. Did he get mad and say this doesn't work? No! He knew it worked and was tickled that he earned that much money and got a great level of popularity from his book. This process works.

One might ask what if I just sat in my room and dreamed about more money and took no action, would that work? I suppose the answer is yes. However, no-one I've ever heard of has done this to any real degree without taking action. Just make sure that the action is what you want to do.

Here is one. Many famous bands and performers I read about all state something similar. They were obsessed about learning how to play their instrument or sing etc. These people all worked very hard but since it was what they loved doing, it wasn't working hard.

It's a problem we have in society. We are told we have to work very hard. It's just not true. We should be told that we should follow our passions and have a happy life. Sure, I know that everyone who picks up a guitar will not make it in the music business. Every kid that puts on a pair of skates won't be the next hockey star. Here's the fact, some do. Also there are a lot of peripheral businesses that fall under these passions that have nothing to do with performing ... music stores, hockey shops, making or repairing instruments, designing new safer hockey equipment for kids and so on; even writing books about famous people. So what is your passion? Are you willing to follow it?

I had a friend of mine tell me that an idea popped into his head to make money. He told me about it. I knew that he didn't want to work long hours. I reminded him of that. He said that he wanted the business not only to make money but for his kids. This concerns me. You see, you have no idea if the kids will follow through on this or not. Their passions may not follow the same path. I didn't really tell him this though. I have a strong feeling that if he does start this business, he will be able to sell it later for a nice profit. The main point I'm making is that you follow your passions and don't worry about others following in your footsteps. You can only control the way you feel not what someone else feels. You also can't follow someone else's passion. Sorry dad, I am proud of what you do but it just doesn't excite me.

Some folks will tell me that they have no particular passion. "MW, what do I do"?

Then approach it from a different perspective. Where would you like to work? At home or a particular company? What lights you up? How many hours a day or a week do you want to work? So if the answers were something like this … I want to work from home in a business that doesn't take more than 5 hours a day or less; I want flexibility to be able to travel and work from wherever I am … Ok, you are talking about a web based or online business. If you are a great writer then write from the beach. No problem. There are simply tons of things you can do online. Think of it this way. If you bought 50 programs teaching you how to make money online and you closed your eyes and pulled one from the pile, you will be very successful. Using these techniques how can't you? If you are excited about making money online and are willing to do everything the teacher tells you to do then you have to be successful.

If you want to work from home in any number of businesses you sure can do so. You could do consultant work. You can build things. You can learn various healing techniques and work by phone or Skype with anyone in the world.

I just want to remind you of something. If you work in an area that depends on you to make money then you are limited in the amount of money you can make. If that amount of money is enough for you then my friend you just hit the jackpot. Nothing wrong with that.

I could do EFT or tapping for a living. Depending on where I am I could do this and earn $100 or more an hour. I think some folks are getting closer to $200 per hour. Multiply that by the number of hours you want to work a week and there's your income. Does that give you everything you want? If so congratulations!

Can your vocation be duplicated? If you are a consultant, can you train others to do the same tasks and have them do the bulk of the work for you? In doing this you can retire and have offices all over the place.

Again with tapping, I was considering this option. I would start the business and then train others in my methods and have them work with me. Then train someone else and so on until I could retire.

Another thought for some people is network marketing. These businesses have been around for decades. Some cost you a monthly fee either in money or product purchases. Again this is something that doesn't light me up in any way. However, a lot of people do make a lot of money in these ventures. The other good side is you get to associate with like-minded people who are passionate about what they do.

I am currently studying a guy who talks about offshore banking. No, it's not illegal or at least it doesn't have to be. I haven't decided if I will buy his program and go all the way with it yet or not. I sure find it interesting. This is a new concept to me. It doesn't mean it's a bad concept, just a new one. Remember those wonderful words? I don't know what I don't know. Maybe he will teach me a new way to make money that will light me up.

I have just finished reading Rich Dad Poor Dad and not for the first time. It's a great book. He made a lot of money by purchasing real estate. This interests me. I own some land now and I will build some apartments for people and charge them a little less than they would normally pay for the same place. In this I will be giving people who can't afford a few nicer features a better home. I will be improving their quality of life and making some money too. Perfect!

There are a lot of lessons in that book. I will be reading it several more times over the next several months.

Don't ever stop reading and learning. Keep growing and watch for the nudges to lead you down the right trail for you.

For me, it isn't all about the money. You know I love teaching this information. I also get excited about making the deal work. If I do get into playing with real estate, the buying and selling properties probably won't light me up. It's making the deal, the winning or not. Watching it all work out. Yes, playing the game. Of course, the whole learning process as well. Just like every time I give a talk about this information I grow, then I will grow through learning a new process like real estate or off shore banking.

Just make sure you know the information in this book before you start reading other books. I know, I've said it throughout this book. Read this book over and over. One hundred times and then again. Get

CHAPTER 18

EFT- Emotional Freedom Technique

As promised, I will tell you a bit about Emotional Freedom Technique, known as EFT or more simply as tapping. I have studied many people but I believe the grandfather of tapping is Gary Craig. He is the one I studied the most.

Years ago he had a 3 library set of DVDs converted from videos. I understand he has a more modern site and you can purchase his program at a very reasonable cost. I can't say enough about Gary. I think he is just an amazing person. Anyone can learn this technique; my feeling is he is the best teacher as he really cares. On top of all that, he is simply a very nice person.

What is tapping?

Tapping is like the acupuncture of emotions. You use your fingers to tap on various acupuncture points that are close to the surface of the skin. While tapping you also say things, affirmations some call them. The procedure is simple and is the most effective method I know for reducing blocks to success, illnesses, negative feelings, or anything negative at all.

You must have a tool like this to reach high levels of success. There are other tools out there but I believe this is the most simple and easy to apply wherever you are. I won't argue this with anyone. The point is to learn a technique that works for you. This is the one I've chosen.

Who Uses Tapping?

The interesting fact is, many people who make a living from tapping were or are in the mental health business; Psychiatrists and other similar fields. During my studies, I have heard several classically trained doctors state that they will use tapping 100% of the time because it works. Clinical psychiatry doesn't have nearly the success rate. The results will last forever and the time to make progress can be as short as a few minutes. Some issues may take a few sessions but it is worth it. I haven't been to Gary Craig's site in some time now but I think he has a list of practitioners who have some accreditation from taking his course.

There are many things you can eliminate on your own. However, working with someone else may be required. I have worked with many people who have had issues in wide ranging areas from sexual assault to muggings to physical illnesses to removing blocks to success. There's a lot of things in-between as well.

I think it is safe to say that we all know that stress is the number one killer. Tapping removes stress beautifully. I think that if everyone took just 5 minutes before bed and tapped on anything that bothered them that day, we would be a much happier race. I know we would sleep better.

I will tap with my one-on-one clients but I choose not to do this for a living. I am a teacher of information. That is my choice. However, I did consider tapping with people as a wonderful way to make a living. To be a healer I guess you might say.

Again, I suggest that you get on my mailing list. I will hold various webinars and seminars and I will likely put in a tapping component for illustration purposes and work with someone in the group. It is fun to do.

Focusing just on the theme of this book, how to dream, believe and achieve whatever you want, here is how tapping can help you. I have worked with quite a few people who have beliefs passed on to them by well-meaning people. Maybe Grandma said that wealthy people are bad. Maybe Dad talks about the rich boss who drives a fancy car thanks to my work, what a jerk.

A lot of people carry around beliefs that they aren't worthy or can't have wealth or even something as simple as love. We were told things in the heat of anger that just aren't true. These become the writing on our walls.

The writing on your wall is things that people have said and they are still there for years and years. They hold you back. We must release these horrible things from our wall. The big powerful eraser is tapping.

Often, addictions stem from the writing on our walls ... food addictions, even drugs and alcohol. More writing that needs to be erased.

I firmly believe that everyone can dream, believe and achieve whatever they want. There are two things that can and will stop us. One is learning how to think. This book teaches you that. The other is the various blocks we have like I'm not good enough to have love, I'm too stupid to be wealthy, and many more. If you don't remove these blocks, I doubt that you can ever be truly happy and have all the things you want in life.

Carol Locke is an EFT master. I love her voice. You can hear that she cares about people and the work that she does. You can find her online as well. She has programs that you can buy that take you through various sequences. She has worked with various LOA folks and created programs to address the more common issues that come up during the learning process. I have an e-book and audios I purchased from her. I can just play the audios and tap along with her. Hey Carol, if you see this plug join me on stage sometime. You too Gary. Grin.

I may have some videos on my membership site demonstrating tapping and some tap along videos but in the meantime check out Carol Locke and Gary Craig.

No matter what, you must have some sort of releasing technique to remove those blocks that will come up. Another technique I have only slightly studied is the Sedona method. Some favor this method over tapping. As I said, I won't argue one over the other. I just happen to know a great deal more about tapping and I have seen the results I get from it. I suggest you do some research and see what best suits you.

Happy tapping and may your wall be filled with good and loving sayings.

Dream, believe and you will achieve whatever you want.

CHAPTER 19

Closing Words

You know I'm going to say it so I will say it right now. This book never ends. When you get to the last word, take a break, write down the date in your binder and then start this all over again. Believe me, you haven't got it. You don't know everything in this book. You need to master this information not just view it as a good read. Those that master this information will be the ones who will make the difference. I really want you to be one of those people. I want to hear of all the wonderful things that have happened in your life since you started applying everything here in these pages.

Something I would like you to do. Please go to http://www.loasecret.com and sign up for my email list. I plan to have a lot of content to help you in your journey. I will be recording videos, audios, have podcasts and probably stuff on YouTube as well. Then there are the webinars and the seminars. Signing up for my emails will enable me to keep in touch with you about all the things I am doing and be able to help you.

Another thing I ask you to please do for me. Can you please go to Amazon and do a review about this book? Even if for some reason your review wouldn't be that great I still ask you to do so. Your honesty and integrity is all I ask for. Thank you for that.

Before I close this off I want to tell you about one of my clients. Her story is a bit different. It touched me in that she is so lovely. I don't think she has a selfish bone in her body. I'm sure that you will agree.

She had various goals that she wanted to achieve. She chose one and it came to be. Then she started working on this one. Her father was getting older and was ill. She wanted to be back in her home town for him and an aging aunt as well. In order to do this she needed to move across the country and needed a new job.

She didn't know how this would all work out. We talked every few weeks and I helped her understand the process. She learned the 4 keys and learned to think of them during the day.

The 4 keys was a big factor in her being successful. She learned who to listen to and who not to listen to. She learned to change her thinking and to not dwell on the negative things. She learned to not focus on the how but just watch for opportunities and act on them when they came up for her.

She had a co-worker who made the job quite miserable. I believe she also had some sort of vandal damage done to her car during that time. This was just more proof of her focusing on the negative in her life and not the positive. She is such a kind and gentle person and I could not stand hearing of these things that were happening to her. It really broke my heart.

At least in this stage of her life she is not looking for great wealth or fancy cars and material things. She just wants to be closer to her family to help them. She wants to spend time with her father before he passes.

I don't know all the details of how things actually ended up coming together for her but I do know that she is going home. She will be able to be with her father.

This wonderful lady has reached her success. By her definition. She has achieved her dream. She indeed learned how to dream, believe and achieve what she wanted and allowed it to come true. I am so very proud of her. I just know that she will be able to do anything she wants from now on. I have no doubt if you have been applying what you have learned in this book that you are seeing manifestations of your dreams coming true already. Just know that it will get better and better as you learn more and more and apply what you learn that your dreams will all come true and you can enjoy a happy life full of love, and success in whatever that means to you.

Embrace and love the learning process. Be obsessed about learning and be amazing!

Dream, believe and you will achieve whatever you want.

AUTHORS NOTE

Michael Winegarden is blind and almost deaf. He has made his dreams his beliefs, and his beliefs his achievements. He lives with the love of his life and together they pursue the dream of happiness. Watch for the next book in which Michael will explore loving relationships.